Baguette Pissant Independence

Additional copies may be ordered from the publisher for educational,
business, promotional or premium use.
For information, contact ALIVE Book Publishing at:
alivebookpublishing.com

Book design by Alex P. Johnson

ISBN 13
978-1-63132-235-8
Library of Congress Control Number: 2024910667

Library of Congress Cataloging-in-Publication Data
is available upon request.

First Edition

Published in the United States of America by ALIVE Book Publishing
an imprint of Advanced Publishing LLC
3200 A Danville Blvd., Suite 204, Alamo, California 94507
alivebookpublishing.com

PRINTED IN THE UNITED STATES OF AMERICA

10 9 8 7 6 5 4 3 2 1

Baguette
Pissant
Independence

Mai McBride

ABOOKS
Alive Book Publishing

To my father, a grain of sand,
who made me become another grain of sand.
Thank you!

Introduction

Who am I? Well, I am merely a Vietnamese woman who has lived under five different regimes: Monarchy, First Republic, Second Republic, Socialist, and in the United States of America. I just want to express what I had ingrained deeply in my mind about my country, my compatriots, with my lonely, silent love.

I also have unanswered questions for all foreigners who came to my homeland in a different period, to exercise their power on the life of my people. Had the Americans not intervened, we would have had our own general election in 1956. There would have been a winner and a loser, but we would not have borrowed foreigners' knives to slaughter each other, our blood would not have been shed, and more than fifty thousand American soldiers would not have spilled their blood on "A damn little pissant country," as a former American president repeatedly referred to Vietnam.

I have asked myself many times: As a powerful country, why was the U.S. Government hellbent on destroying us, even though we are Communist country?

What I tell you here is my own truth—my painful experiences, troubling worries, and my own dreams for the future of my country. The people involved who did wrong, I shall not name as they might be alive or dead. Those who are still alive, if they read these words, I hope they reflect upon themselves and repent. To the deceased, I forgive them. I lead a hatred-free life because I think a hateful attitude will only bring me pain.

MY STORY

Childhood

I was the eldest daughter. When I was two, my younger brother was born, and the following year, another brother. What started to become permanent in my subconscious only happened after I was a little older. My parents took many jobs just to make a living, from wholesaling and retailing bread from a large bakery, to giving injections to patients that were prescribed by doctors. After hours of demanding work, my mother, father, grandmother, and many family friends whom I call uncles, often gathered at our house to play music and sing along. The songs they sang were solemn. I did not see them laughing or telling jokes — only whispers. To a child like me, the music that I had heard repeatedly soon become familiar, but I cannot recall the lyrics. However, there is one piece of music that has, for some mysterious reason, been ingrained in my brain. If I close my eyes, I can still hear the melody, but only a few of the lyrics remain in my mind: "Where Have Our Old Friends Gone?"

On bread retail days, some customers would come to my house to pick up orders, and the rest were delivered by my parents. When my mother gave birth to her third child, she often stayed at home because my grandmother could not manage all the housework alone. Moreover, my mother had to give injections to patients when they could not wait for my father. It is worth noting that to reduce my mother and grandmother's workload while they were looking after me, my father would take me with him on his delivery route. I still clearly remember the shape of his bicycle with the bamboo basket strung on the back, and a small seat in the front designated just for me.

Whenever we went to deliver bread, I paid close attention to my father's arrangement. First, he would put unknown boxes at the bottom of the bamboo basket and then the bread was put on top. At a certain location, my father would pull over to give the boxes under the bread to a stranger, which was a different person each time. The two of them would whisper a few words of exchange and then off we went.

Sometimes it was the other way around. Strangers would give my father something, and he would put it in the bottom of the basket and then return home. When my mother greeted him, they would whisper. My mother would then help to set the bread out on a small table in front of the house to sell to passersby. I could not always go with my father, and he did not always deliver bread. Sometimes he would carry many boxes with syringes and needles inside. I had no idea who they were for since most patients in need of injections would come to our house. Patients said that my parents were virtuous, and that their injections would rid them of diseases quickly. I was not entirely sure if I believed it, but as my grandmother told me later, my parents gave those injections for an unbelievably cheap price, sometimes even giving them away for free to help people in need.

Over time, my family continued business as usual. My parents still sold bread and gave injections to patients, and people continued to come to the house to play music and sing. I was still happy to deliver bread with my dad, but one day, something was unusual; only one uncle showed up at my house. My grandmother moved me and my two brothers to the back of the house, and no one sang; only whispers. After that, when the uncle left, my parents whispered some more, and there was no laughter at dinner as usual. Then before bedtime, my father called me over with a grim expression I had never seen before. He stroked my hair gently and softly spoke to me.

"You are the eldest sister, so you have to set an example for your younger brothers. Be nice, and help your mother and grandmother. Do you understand?"

I was excited to be given responsibility, which meant I was an adult. "Yes, I understand," I quickly replied.

The next day while my father was away, an uncle who frequently came to our house and used to tell me jokes and give me candy, came over. Only this time, he did not pay any attention to me. He just whispered to my mother and left in haste. Right after that, my mother whispered something to my grandmother, who called me and my two brothers to the front yard, and made sure that we stayed there and didn't go the back of the house.

I forgot to mention that as a child, I was always curious about adults. I always paid attention to what was going on around me and asked questions. Often I would get scolded, being told that children should only listen, not ask, and sometimes not even listening was allowed, especially to the whispers of adults.

With my two brothers keeping my grandma busy, I rushed to the back of the house to witness a scene that terrified me. My mother was sitting in front of a metal barrel with a rooster image on its side, the kind that stored kerosene to light stoves and lamps. My grandmother would wash it to use as a rubbish bin once the kerosene ran out. Fire crackled out of the barrel in clouds of smoke. In my mother's hands was a stack of paper that she separated into parts and put in the fire. Just then my grandmother, who had noticed my absence, knowing full well my curious nature, rushed in and dragged me back to the front yard. That night my father did not come home.

In the days during my father's absence, my mother continued with her daily work with more difficulty. My mother did not smile. At dinner, she would often tell Grandma, "You and the kids eat first, I'm not hungry."

I wondered about my father's absence. When I asked, Grandma said that my father was away on a business trip and would return in a few days' time. I do not remember how long it was, but one day my father returned with a battered face, footsteps heavy, leaning against the arms of an uncle who often visited our home. When he got to the door, my father fell to his knees.

My mother hugged him and sobbed. I cried as well, out of fear. My two brothers looked at me in confusion, while my grandmother embraced us in her arms.

I remember asking my mother why my father was in such pain. She said he tripped and fell. I thought father and I were alike. When going out, I often fell on the ground because of carelessness. My grandmother always had to remind me that a lady should walk with caution and look carefully ahead and at the ground so I would not bump into a tree or fall into a hole. I wondered why she had not taught my dad the same thing so he would not fall like that.

Since that day, my father stopped delivering the bread; he simply lay in his room all day. My grandmother told us to keep quiet so that my father could rest. Sometimes he would emerge from the room and call for us. He would pat our heads, eyes distant, and smile gently when my baby brother made a face. Laughter no longer resounded in my house like before and the uncles no longer came to sing along. A few would visit from time to time, but simply to check on my father's condition. The bicycle left against a corner almost seemed miserable because my father never touched it again since he came back. The strangest thing was that every day my grandmother would cook some kind of medicine with a rather dreadful smell in a clay pot. My father had to drink this black concoction every day. He would sometimes refuse to take it, perhaps because of its excessive cost. My grandmother sometimes coaxed, sometimes threatened.

"Drink it to stay alive for the children," my grandmother would say. "Your wife cannot afford to take care of them all. The most I can do is help around the house, but not make money."

After a while, my family left the Ban Co-Vuon Chuoi Market area and moved to a faraway place, at least to me at the time. This area is called Bay Hien Crossroads. Since my family was Catholic, my parents bought a house on the road to Chi Hoa Church. The house was made of palm leaves and bamboo; at night I could see the stars in the sky. On rainy days, it was fun to catch the rain leaking through the roof. What fascinated me was that the neighborhood was spacious and many kinds of fruit trees grew there.

There was a well in the front yard that was always full, but my brothers and I were not allowed to go near it. Once my grandma finished taking the water, she would close it with a big wooden lid. Every morning, I would go to the well to pick up the guavas and plums left on the lid by the birds. They were sweeter and more fragrant than the ones bought at the market. I liked to think that the birds knew I enjoyed the fruit, so they decided to share them with me. Otherwise, why wouldn't they eat all of it?

The neighbors said my house was fortunate to have a freshwater well, for it was rare for the water to be safe to drink in the neighborhood because of mineral contamination. Whenever I drank, I would try to drink it sip by sip to see if it was fresh. Turned out it was just like any old rainwater.

The piece of land next to my house belonged to Mrs. Ba. Her son was the rector of the church, and it seemed that they both were revered by everyone in the village. To be honest, to this day I cannot grasp the title of rector and how reverent it must have been. Whenever Mrs. Ba went to Mass, she would sit right in the front, the seat reserved for the priest's relatives. Only pious people loved by God could sit where the "Lord dwells." My family had to sit in the last row. Mrs. Ba's house also had a freshwater well like ours, but that water was reserved to water her betel vine business, keeping her garden green and lush.

One day when she was away, a neighbor came to take a handheld bucket of water from her well to drink since it was only one bucket. I was sure because I was playing in the front yard when the neighbor came over and I saw everything. As I have said, I was curious by nature. When Mrs. Ba came back to find out someone had stolen water from her well, she cursed the whole neighborhood out since she could not find the culprit. She was screaming her lungs out for a long while until she finally ran out of breath, totally forgetting that she was supposedly a child of God, the mother of the rector, and the exemplary follower of the parish. That night I could not stop thinking about a question in my mind. After dinner, I approached my grandma while she was knitting.

I asked, "Why would Mrs. Ba, a child of God, not forgive a neighbor for taking a bucket of water? Wouldn't it be a sin for her to curse like that?"

Grandma answered, "That is not for you to judge." Her voice turned solemn. "It is between her and the Lord. As for us, we will tell the neighbors to come here if they need water, alright?"

"Yes, Grandma," I softly replied. That is what I said, but I could not help but feel frustrated. Why would a child of God be so selfish and horrible?

Since then, if anyone in the neighborhood needed water, they would come to our house at any time. When people drew the water, the well looked empty, but the water always would fill up again by the next morning. To me, it was a miracle. I heard others talking about how my family was blessed, and that we would come to have great fortune. Needy people came to us to get injections, and now the neighbors came to get water, but I still was not sure what "blessings" and "fortune" meant.

"Grandma," I asked one day. "What is great fortune?"

She thought for a moment. "Great fortune will come when we love and help others," she replied, speaking slowly. "Heaven and earth will remember our good deeds, and when we're in need, God will let others help us."

I was glad because that way, my father's ailment would soon be gone. God will send someone to help him because my family had "great fortune." For that, I would gladly wait.

Although my father did not get out much, many friends would come to visit him. Gone was the singing like in the old days. They would just whisper for a long time, and I would have to hang out in the yard with my brothers instead of listening. The place we were living in then was different from the place before. After 5 p.m., everyone had to stay inside.

At the end of the street in front of my house was Chi Hoa Church. Next to the church was a primary school taught by nuns. Both the church and the school campus were under the control of the Black mar-ac (French Moroccan soldiers). Every morning on our way to Mass, my grandma would get up early. But when we got there, if it was not time, we had to sit on the ground in front of the barbed wire gate and wait. The mar-ac soldiers would shine a searchlight from their high watchtower to check who we were, though they saw us every day. The light was blinding. My grandmother always told us to sit still and let them check. The adults said that our church was located near a mar-ac's ammunitions depot, so they checked everything. I thought to myself, "Who would take their ammo to warrant all that strict security?"

My brothers had lots of colorful bullets (in Vietnamese the word bullets have the same meaning as marbles). When the uncles came by to visit my father, they would bring us gifts: marbles for my two brothers and a blue-eyed doll for me. We were adjusting to our new life in what my grandmother called, "a peace of mind."

One midday, my father was lying on his bed. He was so thin that at a glance, he seemed to disappear into the blankets and pillows. Suddenly, men wearing strange clothes burst into the house with guns and asked for my father. My mother was away, so my grandmother pointed to the room where he was lying. They barged into the room, shouting things I could not understand. Someone dragged my father out of bed and threw him on the ground like a rag. He groaned in pain. I ran to cover him, to protect him. I begged them not to hit him. They rummaged through the house, even upturned the kitchen; rice and food was spread all over the ground. (The house was built on dirt, with no floor cover).

After they left, Grandma asked me to help father to bed. For a moment, I saw blood coming out of his mouth. She told me to go grab a towel to wipe up the blood. I trembled in fear and ran to pick up a towel thrown on the ground by those strangers. Once I gave it to Grandma, I burst into tears. My father whispered to me, telling me to go comfort my brothers and let him rest for a while. I complied, but truthfully, I just wanted to stay by his side.

One night, the family was shaken from sleep by the sound of gunfire and shouting, footsteps on the ground, then silence. My two brothers and I went back to sleep but my parents and grandma stayed awake, whispering. The next morning, Grandma, my two brothers, and I, were getting ready to go to Mass as usual when suddenly there was someone's panicked screaming. My grandmother decided we would just stay home to read the bible. When the sun was high in the sky, a neighboring couple ran over to give my family an update. They whispered, but it was loud enough for me to hear.

"Last night, two strangers were discovered by the ma-rocs in our area. One got shot. His body is still there, and no one has claimed it yet. The other was wounded but managed to escape. The ma-rocs are chasing him now. We heard that the two men were planning to destroy the ammo depot."

They paused for a moment, and then the couple looked at each other.

"I think the man who was killed is one of your acquaintances," the woman whispered. "Why don't you come check the body to see if you know him? We've seen that man around your house many times."

"Don't be ridiculous," my mother interrupted, her voice stern. "You must have been mistaken. Please leave. If this got out, we would be in trouble."

My mother went back inside and the couple turned away, still mumbling under their breath. I didn't know what would happen next, but the questions were already forming in my inquisitive mind. "Who were those two men? Why was one of them shot dead?" Mother said, "Children should not meddle with adults' business."

That night, my father joined the family for dinner. In truth, he was only half sitting, half lying, on a folding chair next to us. He had not eaten for a long time; he only took medicine. The kerosene lamp in the middle of the table was not bright enough for my father to look at everyone, so my grandmother put my little brother on her lap to make room for the light to illuminate where my father lay. He looked at my youngest brother with a gentle smile.

"This kid eats well and sleeps well. No wonder he is chubby," my father said. "His brother is a fussy eater, so he is thin. And this girl (me) is always asking and asking. No wonder you cannot grow any inches."

My mother smiled a sad smile at my father, and then gave him a bowl with a spoonful of rice and some soup.

"Have some rice with the family," she said gently to him. My father pushed himself up to take the bowl.

"Yeah, I'm feeling well today, so maybe an extra bowl after this one," he replied.

I was overjoyed. My father was getting better for sure. He would get better because our family had "great fortune." But for some reason, I saw tears in my mother's eyes. She hastily turned away, so I must have imagined it. When my father was halfway through finishing his bowl, hurried footsteps resounded inside our house. In the blink of an eye, our house was once again filled with uninvited men in strange clothes. This time they wore Ao Ba Ba (a traditional southern Vietnamese garment) and Non-La (palm-leaf conical hat), and had guns in their hands.

They asked for the name and location of a person. When my father said he did not know, they dragged him up and hit him square in the chest with the hilts of their guns. My father fell to the ground. The rice bowl shattered. They stepped over my father's crumbled body and continued with their raid. They finally left, but with a warning to return. Mother and Grandma took my father to his room. I picked up the broken pieces of the rice bowl and cleaned up the spilled food. What surprised me was that I did not cry. Anger filled me, bubbling up and sticking in my throat. "Why do people keep hurting my father?" I asked myself, bewildered.

As I passed my father's room, I heard my grandma's voice:

"It was the French. They were disguised in black Ao Ba Ba clothing."

After I finished cleaning, I put my brothers to bed and tucked them in while Grandma and Mother were still in the room with Father. Fear followed me to sleep like a nightmare. Early in the morning, my grandma woke me from my sleep. She said that my father wanted to talk to me. I jumped out of bed quickly and ran to my father's room. There, my mother was crying—weeping, with tears rolling down her cheeks incessantly. Father was leaning on a folding chair. He asked me to stand next to him and gestured to my mother to help him stand up. Suddenly, he fell to his knees and bowed to my grandmother three times.

"If I have done anything to upset you," he said to Grandma, "please forgive me. Please take care of my three children no matter what." With tears in her eyes, my grandmother helped my father back to his chair.

"I promise," she said, voice broken. "Do not worry."

Taking a deep breath, my father asked me to come to him. He reached out his thin, trembling hand to hold mine. He looked at me, eyes full of love.

"Daddy is going away," he breathed. "You won't be able to see me anymore."

I burst into tears. I screamed. I stomped. I held onto

my father's arm. "No! No!" I sobbed. "Please stay. I won't talk too much. I won't meddle with adults' business. Daddy, don't go. Do not leave me. Grandma, Mom, tell him."

Father waited until my outburst subsided. Then he looked into my eyes.

"I'm glad that as a person, you can feel deep within your heart," he told me with a solemn voice. (He saw that I did not understand). "What I meant," he continued, "was that it's okay to shed a few tears whenever you feel sad and down. But you need to think and come up with something to rid yourself of your misery. Tears alone will not do. When I am gone, you must share the burden with your grandma and take care of your brothers. Mother will bring home the bacon, so as the eldest daughter, I give that responsibility to you. Even when you can no longer see me, trust that I am always with you. Can you promise me that?"

"I promise," I said to mollify him, but in truth, all I wanted was for him to stay, bedridden or otherwise.

"The last and most important thing I need to tell you," he continued, voice breathy, "is that not only do you need to take care of your grandma and two brothers, but when you grow older, you have to care for our nation and our people. Can you promise me that as well?"

"I do, but I don't even know what those words mean. How can I care for them?" I asked as he squeezed my hand.

"You are my daughter. In time, you will surely

understand. Now go. Your brothers need breakfast, and you need to go to school."

"Yes, Daddy," I replied, and ran out to my brothers. I wanted to show my father that I would comply with anything he asked of me.

The following morning, the church bells rang, one by one, when I was sitting in class. To Catholics, this meant a member of the parish had just passed away. My instincts told me it was my father. I was terrified, but no tears came. A while later, my grandma came to ask permission to take me home because my father had passed. I followed in her hurried footsteps, muttering,

"Don't worry, Grandma, I'll help you take care of my brothers."

My dad was buried on a rainy day because the uncles who came to help us could not wait. "We have to leave as soon as possible," they said.

The sound of the raindrops could not cover the sound of our sobbing. The uncles carried the coffin, and we followed on foot to the cemetery; only us, no neighbors, might be because of the rain?

A few days following my father's funeral, the ammo depot near the church exploded. Burning fragments of ammunition fell like rain onto our house. With no better way to protect us, my grandmother told all three of us children to lie down on the ground, and then she laid on top. If the shrapnel hit, she would shield us with her body. Fortunately, the shrapnel only left a burn on her heel; the rest of us were unharmed.

From that day, I became an adult in the body of a five-year-old. I took care of my brothers from their meals to their studies. My grandmother did not need to worry. But there were two things lingering in the back of my mind: Why was my father tortured, despite our "good fortune," and why did my grandma refuse, every time I asked her, to sing the song with the phrase, "Where Have Our Old Friends Gone?" because I missed my father so much.

"Don't ask," she said curtly. "Can't sing. Don't remember."

I knew for a fact she remembered, because back in the days when people visited our home, my father would play the banjo, my mother the mandolin, and Grandma would sing. I hated that I could not remember more of the words and melody.

Just like my father said, after his passing, my mother was often away for work. As for me, after finishing the housework, I often wandered into the rubber tree forest alone to collect firewood for cooking. The neighborhood children would refuse to play with me, for reasons I could not understand. Once I asked, and a neighbor kid told me his parents would not allow it. And when I went to confession, the priest told me to pray so that when I grew up, I would not be like my parents. What did that even mean? According to Grandma, my father has "good fortune," so now he is in heaven with God, so why did the priest tell me not to be like him?

Sometimes when I missed my father, I would lay on the grass, looking up at the cloudy sky, in the hope that I could see my father up in heaven. When I could not see him in the sky, the priest's words rang again in my head. Maybe my father was a bad person so he couldn't go to heaven. But I wanted to be like him no matter what. Torn between God, the priest, and my father, I could no longer experience the joy of childhood. Sadness weighed heavily in my heart. I talked less and preferred to keep to myself in my thoughts.

I cannot recall exactly when, but one day my mother told me to dress all of us in formal attire. We took a horse carriage to a residential area like where we lived before, then switched to a motorcycle. My brothers and I were very excited; it was our first-ever outing. We came to an old house on an exceptionally large piece of land. Rusty inoperative machinery covered with dust littered the area. I could not tell what they were. We continued walking through a rusted gate where an elderly woman was waiting. My mother bowed, and then she turned to us: "Come greet your paternal grandmother."

We did as we were told, but I was beyond shocked because I had been told that the grandmother on my father's side passed away when he was young. I had never met her, so what does this mean? I looked closely; her hair was almost white, her face seemed solemn, but her smile was gentle. Her posture seemed tough. She wore a white, short-sleeved Ao Ba Ba. She patted our heads and led us inside, where she pointed to a table full of fruit and candies.

"Help yourselves," she told us softly. "I will pack some for you to bring home too."

With that, she took my mother to the next room, and

I knew that the exchange in that room was adults' business. My brothers were ecstatic to gobble down what was in front of us. It had been a while since we had this kind of food. I just ate a few bites. I was more interested in the relationship between Grandma and us.

The things I overheard from my mother and Grandma's exchange shook me to my core. From what I remember that day, my mother came to ask for permission to move and pursue a different life. She said my father gave his life to revolution, and it was too hard for her to raise all of us alone, and the worst thing was that people shunned us. They were lifelong parishioners while my family were converted Catholics. They did not like people like us. Grandma comforted my mother and spoke with sympathy in her voice. She handed my mother a small bag with some money that Dad's comrades saved up to help us. I walked back to where my two brothers were still eating treats from the table.

Questions filled my mind: Who exactly was that grandmother, who were the comrades, what did she mean my dad gave his life to revolution, and what are converted Catholics?

It was not until the end of primary school that my grandmother explained to me why we were Catholic. Originally, my family worshiped ancestors. My grandma was the youngest in a family of six children. My great-grandparents died young when my grandma was little, and the rest of her siblings had their own families so no one took on the responsibility of raising her. They sent her to a convent until she was eighteen, provided, of course, that she converted to Catholicism. In addition to that, my grandma learned both Vietnamese and French, embroidery, and sewing. She was the one who taught us how to read, write, and do math before we started kindergarten, especially sewing and embroidery on my part.

My grandmother was a model Catholic, but it was strange how she always taught us to follow God, and not priests. "The closer we are to priests, the further we stray from God," she said. I could not understand her then, but now with more life experience, I finally realized how deep that teaching was. One mystery was solved, but why my father was killed, his comrades also killed, and the grandmother on father's side, all remained unknown.

Farewell My Childhood!

Two years after my dad died, my mother decided to move closer to the city. We bid farewell to Chi Hoa—farewell to the place that held the last memories of my dad, farewell to his final resting place, farewell to the fruit trees my grandma had planted, farewell to the well that gave us fresh water, farewell to the birds and their sweet guava and plums they shared with me, and farewell to my childhood.

We moved to a tiny house facing Tan Phuoc Street, No. 184, near Nguyen Tri Phuong Market. My mother said we were lucky to own this house despite not having much money because houses like this usually cost a lot. The house was on the market for a long time, but no one was interested. Rumor has it that the house was haunted. The owner of the house killed herself with a fetus still in her womb, leaving behind three young children. She did it as a wake-up call for her husband who was addicted to betting on horse races, neglecting his wife and children to starve because he gambled his salary away. With her warning falling on deaf ears, she chose death so that her three children could live.

That was the first time I realized the evil parts of society. At my age at that time, going to school and helping my grandmother raise my brothers was all I knew, but from stories I gathered from adults, the country was in chaos. Factions fought for rights. Casinos, brothels, and other debauchery sprang up. Beggars with open wounds or just pretending, gathered in markets if begging did not work and they harassed people. That situation has always terrified me. Every day when I went to school, I had to pass by a very sketchy neighborhood. Instead of houses, they had shelters patched with pieces of tar paper and rusty tin sheets. They lived by digging through dumpsters for bottles, food, and leftover fruit like orange and tangerine peels, and durian and jackfruit seeds, which they dried under the sun and then resold.

The First Republic

One day, a priest from overseas was rumored to be returning to save the country. Then people distributed leaflets with photos of King Bao Dai and a priest named Ngo Dinh Diem, saying everyone had the right to vote. No one knew who Mr. Diem was, only that he was from Central Vietnam and was Catholic. The public was fed up with the current state of society. They wanted a change, and hoped the priest would save society from its ills. I was not sure about the results, but he was declared the winner and became the president of the South.

The authorities gave us new songs to learn by heart. At school, after the national anthem, we had to sing about the president's merits. At movie theaters, before the movie started, we had to salute the flag and pay our respects to the president. Madame Tran Le Xuan, the wife of Ngo Dinh Nhu, who was Diem's brother, imposed a law banning divorce. Statues of the legendary Trung sisters were created with Madame's face. The scary thing was that Mr. Nhu's secret service did not spare those who dared to speak out.

In Vinh Long, Bishop Ngo Dinh Thuc (Diem's brother) controlled parishioners and the entire government in the South. Officials had to run whatever they wanted to do first through the bishop. His power was no secret. The convoy of important officials that came to Vinh Long to meet with him alone made that more than obvious. In the Central Vietnam, Ngo Dinh Can (Diem's brother) was the king of the realm. The rulings of an uncouth man with many bizarre indulgences also terrified the people. I do not know about others, but my family lived in anxiety. Widespread poverty continued. Many more houses on stilts were built along the stinking canals. I was surprised when Saigon was named the "Pearl of the Far East." I thought, by comparison, that the neighboring countries were even worse.

When he was healthy, my father loved to do photography, especially when we were young. He took pictures of everything we did. He also took many photos of friends and relatives and I love looking at them repeatedly. There are over a hundred photos, but I don't seem to get bored seeing them over and over. Whenever I miss my father, I turn to his photos. One day, as usual, I opened the photo box and took each photo out carefully.

As I grew older, I was more attentive to the old photos, and studied each person's face. Suddenly, one photo caught my attention: my father had taken a picture of people holding up a banner that read "Living in Death, Tran Van On," next to a cyclo carrying funeral wreaths. Curiosity led me to dump the entire box on the floor and find about five more pictures. They were taken in the same place, but with separate groups of people. I grabbed a photo and ran to find Grandma to ask her about the meaning of the banner. My grandmother's face turned blue. She snatched the photos from my hands and told me to give them all to her. Then she went to the kitchen and burnt them; thus my question remained unanswered.

At the age of ten, my mother hired a tutor whose name was Mr. Quang to help us with math. Besides schoolwork, Mr. Quang also taught us common courtesy with the people around us. He especially paid attention to me when we learned about patriotism. I listened attentively but did not understand what patriotism was. Mr. Quang was nice despite the hint of sadness, even in his smile. One day, he stopped coming. His friend, Mr. Nam, took over instead. After whispering for a while with my mom, he told us that Mr. Quang was busy on a trip so he had asked Mr. Nam to step in. Mr. Nam was also nice with a hint of sadness like Mr. Quang, also dressed in worn shirts with patches, and rode a rickety old bicycle. After a short while, Mr. Nam, too, stopped coming. My mom said he was busy on a trip, but from what I gathered from her and Grandma's whispers, they both got caught. I cried myself to sleep many nights. I did not understand why they were caught, and by whom. And how did my mother find out?

Roots

After my father's death, my brothers and I visited my great aunt every Tet holiday (Vietnamese New Year). She was my grandfather's sister; it was just the two of them. My grandfather had two children—my father and my uncle, whereas my great aunt had only one son. My uncle and my great aunt's son had gone to an undisclosed place. She just said that one day my uncle and her son would surely return. Then a question popped into my head. I had a lot of distant family members near and far, and they all had loved ones like husbands, children, or brothers who had gone to work far away but had yet to return.

My paternal family came from Bac Ninh (in the northern part of Vietnam) to settle in Cambodia, and my maternal side came from Hue (in the central region of Vietnam), and settled in the same place. When my parents fell in love and planned to get married, they faced lots of obstacles, because my paternal side kept the tradition of ancestor worship, while my maternal side was Catholic. My grandmother only asked for one thing: my father must follow Catholicism. My paternal side's grandfather was strongly against this as my father was the eldest son.

At the time, Vietnamese, Cambodians, and Laotians could travel back and forth across the border freely, so my father often returned to Saigon (Ho Chi Minh City today).

Someone told my grandfather that he saw my father hanging around a bridge over a deep river. The witness warned my grandfather that my father could be thinking of suicide because he could not marry my mother, the most beautiful girl in the province. That report scared my grandfather. To save his son, he allowed him to marry my mother and follow her religion. It was not until later, after my father brought us to live in Saigon, that my grandfather learned that my father's trips to the bridge were to collaborate with those who shared his dream for a better Vietnam and create a plan to make it happen.

Growing up

Before I knew it, I was admitted to Gia Long High School, on my first attempt at the exam. What surprised me was that many moms in the neighborhood came and asked my mom for tips on buying a good score on the exam. Those moms spent a lot, but the tips were a swindle, so their children failed the exam. My mother gave an honest answer, that she was too busy with her business to pay attention to my exams, let alone buy me a passing score. Please note that I am not bragging. I just want to emphasize that buying and selling exams at that time was commonplace.

Entering high school was a step into adulthood. I knew what had been happening across the country. My father was a revolutionist against the French.

Growing up in a middle-class family (my grandfather owned a restaurant and a small motel), he did not fight because of his poverty, but he contributed his life, his family's well-being, and his wealth to the most significant cause: Vietnam's independence. My nation was divided into two parts: the North under the Democratic Republic and the South under the Republic of Vietnam. People in the South flocked to the North to join the army. That was why the men, like my uncle and great aunt's son, had to "work" far away. My teachers,

Mr. Quang and Mr. Nam, were revolutionists against the Americans. My paternal grandmother was a senior who silently ran a business to support revolution. At the same time, I also understood that I had to keep this information to myself for the sake of my family's safety.

I did not know the difference between Communists and Republicans. I only heard radio propaganda from the South that people in the North lived in poverty, were fighting against each other, and that parents, children, brothers, and sisters were killing each other for a bowl of rice. Children did not attend school. Instead, they were bullet shields on the battlefield. Those misleading stories were all we heard.

In the South, mostly in the countryside, I heard that President Diem established strategic hamlets to protect the villagers from being killed at the hands of brutal Communist soldiers, but the people rejected the idea of strategic hamlets. Who were the Communists, and why would they kill people? Why do people refuse help that is for their own protection? There were student demonstrations rumored to be instigated by Communists. Buddhism was suppressed. Monk Thich Quang Duc set himself on fire at the corner of Le Van Duyet and Phan Dinh Phung Streets, followed by many other monk self-immolations from South to Central Vietnam.

A curfew was imposed. Pagodas were attacked. Monks and nuns were arrested in the night. Madame Nhu's reaction to reports of Buddhists rebelling appeared in foreign newspapers which made matters worse. Independence Palace was bombed by one of our own pilots. Generals plotted a coup. People lived in fear of being framed. I remembered my father and Mr. Quang's advice that I must love my homeland, but my homeland was anything but a loveable place. I lived in horror with rumors of violence from the North and turmoil I witnessed in the South. What should I do?

On one particularly melancholy day, I took out a photo of my parents on their wedding day. The strange thing was that while my mother smiled brightly, like that of a newlywed bride, but my father's face was solemn and sad. Why? Father should be happy to marry my mother, but why were his eyes full of concern? I suddenly realized that the sadness in his eyes and face was like that of the old uncles, and like that of Mr. Quang and Mr. Nam. I began to see answers to the questions I had held in my mind since childhood. Dad, uncles, Mr. Quang, and Mr. Nam shared the same worries, the same concerns, and the same ideal, but what was that ideal? I wanted to know.

Out of Poverty

In the past, a mother would feed a newborn child with her own milk. The husband hustled to feed his wife and children, and the wife stayed at home as the homemaker, feeding and raising the children. I'm not sure if it was the financial struggles that made both the husband and wife work, or if the role of women in society had changed, but many women went back to work a few months after childbirth. Then they couldn't breastfeed their babies, so they had to substitute formula for breast milk.

At that time, a large import-export company started importing infant formula made in the U.S. to replace breast milk. For the first time, American products were available in the Vietnamese market to compete with the French. The rich in the South at that time used French formula exclusively, as they had grown used to the presence of French goods. My mother signed a contract with an American company to introduce and distribute their brand of formula for a basic salary plus a percentage of her total sales. The demand was so great, that soon after some promotion, SMA milk powder distributed by my mother surged in the market, and sales rose even without advertising. My mother did not have to work much, yet the company shared profits with her every month according to contracts that she negotiated. In a short time, my mother saved up enough money to buy a house in downtown Saigon so we moved again. Considering her free time and my available help, my mother decided to open a restaurant specializing in Vietnamese food. That restaurant was located opposite the REX cinema, in front of the City Hall on Nguyen Hue Street.

Our "new" home was an old house near Ham Nghi Street next to "the Old Market," famous for its roasted pork, poultry, and freshly baked bread. I often wandered around the bakery; the smell reminded me of the days when I went with my dad to deliver bread and the packages that he hid at the bottom of the woven basket. Beyond this area was the animal market where people bought and sold animals, from dogs and birds of all kinds to monkeys, snakes, and many other species.

In 1963, a major event occurred in the South. The Ngo Dinh Diem regime was overthrown. His brothers were brutally killed, and top generals continued to change their positions. Panic ensued and everyday people yearned for stability, as they do everywhere. In the same year, I finished high school and got married when the First Republic ended.

The Second Republic

Society

After a long fight for power between the generals, in 1967, Mr. Nguyen Van Thieu became the president of the Second Republic. Even though I was busy as a wife and mother, I noticed a change in the air. Nightclubs and bars sprang up on the main streets of the city. The number of the United States military and other countries' armed forces increased day by day. They lived in apartment blocks surrounded by barbed wire and blockhouses with sandbags piled up in front. Those neighborhoods were inaccessible to us.

Two years later, I was pregnant with my second child, and my husband was drafted. Wishing to avoid frontline duty with the army, he seized all my money, jewelry, and dowry, without my consent, to pay his way into a colonel's house as a piano teacher for the colonel's children. So he did not wear a uniform, but still received a salary from the army. That was the beginning of a different kind of enlisted soldier: Linh ma (ghost soldiers: senior military officers submitted names of deceased soldiers to collect their basic pay), and Linh kieng (decorative soldiers: soldiers gave their basic pay to senior military officers so they could continue to live civilian lives).

As the mobilization order was getting stricter and stricter, words like "ghost soldiers" and "decorative soldiers" were added to the language. I do not dare to say it all, but I do confirm that many high-ranking officers up to generals had quite a lot of ghost soldiers and decorative soldiers on their payrolls. Without ghost soldiers and decorative soldiers' money, their salaries were nowhere near enough to provide for weekend fun at the bars, not to mention their lovers and mistresses.

On the other hand, enlisted soldiers also had their share of a corrupted military system. A married soldier got paid for each child he had but his wife did not have to actually give birth. Every year he just submitted a false birth certificate, and five was a suitable number to stop at. That was enough for his family comfort.

There were lots of young men of draft age in the town where I lived. Every month, the police would run house checks to arrest any cases of draft evasion. They had an incredibly special way of doing things that no one could escape from. Usually around midnight when people were asleep, they would park patrol cars at the front of the alley and announce loudly for about five or ten minutes, "Police search." Then they would slowly knock on doors from house to house. Some woke up prepared with their household members' declarations; others took out the money. It was because of their diligent work that the young men of military age in my neighborhood, most of whom were Vietnamese but of Chinese origin, continued to live at home. When they went out, they would always keep a certain amount of money on hand in case they got caught. It was important to possess the right amount. I once asked a neighbor how to know how much was enough and he replied with a smile, "You wouldn't know it, but we have our network."

People in this period got rich fast, especially in the lines of work where money was coming from the U.S. Apart from their salaries, those who worked for American agencies took advantage of buying and selling U.S. dollars in the illegal market; green notes, and red notes. Those who worked as garbage collectors for Americans took advantage of selling discarded items. Americans' leftovers fattened pigs incredibly well. Flea markets on Ky Dong Street sold necessities such as canned food, rice, cooking oil, confections, etc., especially clean second-hand clothes that smelled of American detergents. Only later when I moved to the U.S. did I realize that the necessities sold at the flea market were pulled out of aid packages for the poor sent from the U.S. But our poor received nothing, so some people got rich at the expense of the poor.

There were ways to get rich from all social classes, but the fastest way for the working class was our women selling their bodies to American soldiers. Squalid shacks were quickly demolished and replaced with high-rises with money from sex. Families with many daughters changed their lives in the blink of an eye. I knew a family with five daughters whose parents were addicted to gambling and deep in debt. Their eldest daughter started selling herself to save her siblings. Just a short while after, she had enough money to build a beautiful house for the family and pay off her parents' debts. But as it was too easy to make money, her parents could not rid themselves of their addiction. Her tears were heartbreaking. Soon the remaining siblings followed her, the youngest of which had yet to develop into a woman.

When my mother was still advertising formula milk, she hired a full-time driver and helped him pay for the car rental and to raise a bunch of his children. They were dirt poor. My mother pitched in to help with hospital fees and medicine when the children were sick. When my mother opened her restaurant and stopped using a car, he changed course and started driving prostitutes and their clients from bars to hotels. Bars were the place to find prostitutes, but any further business required a hotel room. At that time, a secretary made three thousand dongs a month, and a girl who sold her body to U.S. soldiers made three thousand dongs per hour.

My mom's former driver, after discussing it with his wife, turned their bedroom into a dirt-cheap room for rent. American soldiers were easygoing, as they only needed a bed for roughly an hour. The driver and his wife, after a long struggle with poverty, were now presented with an opportunity to get rich. He stopped bringing girls and soldiers to his home, but instead just brought the American soldiers. His wife was willingly waiting for the foreign soldiers on their marital bed. One day, my mother and I happened to pass by the area where the driver lived. We did not recognize the once shabby shack, now a three-story house. We thought we had the wrong address, but the driver saw us and hurried out to invite us in warmly, his neck and hands covered in gold jewelry. After some courteous questions, my mother asked him how he got so rich. He smiled as he shamelessly explained, "Auntie, driving just would not cut it. I had to seize my chance. My wife is not getting any younger, and she is not that fit to begin with. They say behind every great man, there is a great woman, no?"

My mother's restaurant was not luxurious but elegant enough. Thanks to the fantastic location, tasty food, and decent service, the restaurant attracted quite a lot of customers, mostly tycoons, moguls of all industries, officials, and newspaper editors. Sometimes patrons quarreled. That was how I found out that there were newspapers with no need for readers; just a license to publish utter garbage was enough. The main profit was from re-selling the paper they were allowed to buy instead of printing actual newspapers.

The war got worse and worse. People lived without knowing what tomorrow would bring. At night, the sound of rockets flying over their heads would let them know they were still alive. During the day, they tried to avoid crowded places for fear of hidden explosives. The economy had completely fallen into the hands of the Chinese. District 5 was their capital. They manipulated the market: hoarding, setting prices. If a corrupt mayor was willing to share the profit, he'd live to get rich. If he was ethical and righteous, he'd soon be replaced.

The demonstrations that emerged were mostly organized by students, and those who attended demonstrations against the regime were labeled Communists. That was the government's way of quelling protests because jail time for public protest is much shorter than for being a Communist. I believe that among those people, some were Communists, but not all. In fact, not many people understood the definition of the two regimes. They just protested to find the right path for the country.

My younger brother reached the age to get drafted. My mother tried to find him a way out because of his illness. As for the youngest, she arranged for him to join the police force so that he did not have to go to the battlefield. My mother was afraid of the war in the South and North; they could kill each other without hesitation. He refused to join the police force.

"People here hate the police," he said. "You have seen how they bully people. Even if I became a good police officer, they would see the uniform from afar and hate me for it. They would not want to get close enough to find out that I'm not like the other police."

So, he joined the army. In 1968, the Year of the Monkey, my youngest brother was stationed in Quang Duc. He worked in an office called financial administration. He was in charge of distributing basic pay to soldiers because he had some academic qualifications. He was sentimental by nature and always helped his comrades in the camp, so he was well liked. At noon on December 31, 1968, he was eating in the club when some soldiers asked him for early pay as they wanted to have a little something for their family to celebrate the New Year. He stopped eating, left the club, and went back to his office to pay those soldiers.

After he finished his work, he returned to the club to finish his meal. On the way back, he heard an old sergeant crying for help. He rushed to check and saw the old sergeant sprawled on the ground being strangled by a mentally ill soldier. He quickly jumped into action and held the soldier so that the sergeant could escape. Others nearby witnessed the attack, but none of them dared to help for fear of the aggression of a lunatic. After the sergeant had gone, my brother gently patted the impaired soldier, released him, and turned to walk away.

Suddenly the violent soldier snatched a gun from the hand of another man standing nearby and pulled the trigger. The bullets struck my youngest brother's head and back. He died instantly. The day the unit returned his belongings to me, besides the radio, there was also a wallet still soaked with his blood. I opened it to find only some loose change and a picture of me and my three children. There was only that one picture because he had no girlfriend.

When my mother and I went to receive his death gratuity, the captain asked my mother if she wanted to sue the soldier who killed my brother. She remained quiet.

"Sir, if we can sue," I answered on her behalf, "we will sue whoever had the responsibility for treating that soldier at a hospital, but chose not to do so. We know this is not the only violent episode. Everyone at the incident was terrified. The commanding officer's many requests to send him to a mental hospital had fallen on deaf ears. We believe that the unfit soldier must have been forced to remain on duty to replace a ghost soldier on a high-ranking officer's payroll. If that is the case, do you think we are capable of such a thing?"

Battles turned fiercer. Wounded soldiers ravaged the city. Barred from dance halls and upscale places by guards, they went to places like my mother's restaurant. We sympathized with their wounds. Every time they came in, we always welcomed them as guests. We never charged them for food. However, they were insatiable. Once, during a lunch rush, we were serving customers when wounded soldiers barged in and demanded to be served first. My mother begged them to let the other customers eat first as they must go back to work.

They refused to listen, snatching the food from my mother's hands and shoving her down. I ran to her side when a wounded soldier held up a grenade and shoved it in my face.

"Little runt," he spat out, "bring the food now, or I'll shoot the hell out of you."

My mother was furious. Unable to restrain herself, she grabbed the grenade, held it up, and told all the diners to run outside at once.

"If you youngsters aren't afraid of dying," she hissed, voice resolute, "what does an old lady like me have to fear? Everyone eventually dies, so are you ready to die with me this very second, right?"

It was beyond my imagination. The troublemakers

scurried to the door, leaving the grenade behind, and never returned. These soldiers were typical of most of the Army of the Republic of Vietnam. They looted livestock and bullied people everywhere they went, even in the city, but they were just cowardly groups. I once heard from an infantry captain that the hardest thing while marching was to keep the soldiers from pillaging, but it was impossible to keep a check on all of them. They just needed a few seconds. Even large livestock like pigs fell victim to out of control troops, let alone chickens and ducks.

Cowardice

When I was pregnant with my fifth child, my mother sold the restaurant. I saved some money and partnered up with a friend to open a small restaurant on Tran Hung Dao Street. The new restaurant started off slow but with potential. I was full of hope thanks to my knack for cooking. Everything went well as the shop was too small to be disturbed by the soldiers. A month after my labor, we had a small party to celebrate. On the way home, I was run down by an Australian military vehicle. The Australian soldiers had just arrived in Vietnam, so they were still driving on the left. I was hurt from head to toe. My left leg snapped in half with flesh and bones sticking out, my right knee was cracked, and the wound on my head was bleeding down my face. I passed out and woke up to find myself in Binh Dan Hospital. They let me lie on the stretcher in a dark corner, blood still gushing out. I was cold and shivering. No one treated me.

When my family came, someone whispered, "Slide them some money and you'll have a blanket." We did as we were told.

"But what about first aid?" my family asked.

"It is late, doctors are sleeping. We cannot wake them up," the nurse answered.

Fortunately, my friend's brother was a doctor at

another hospital, so he came over and woke up the doctor on duty that night. Perhaps due to his sleepiness, the doctor only bandaged me up in a hurry without straightening the bone or cleaning the wound.

A month later, my leg was infected. Pus oozed and I was in terrible pain. The treatment they recommended was to cut my leg off. Terror struck me: If I lost a leg, how would I raise my children? I went to the police station, hoping they had kept a record of who hit me that night. I needed financial help to be treated at a private hospital. To my disbelief, there was no police record of the accident because it was a foreign soldier (police feared foreigners). The Australian soldier did not bother to come back to see if I was alive or dead. I sold everything I could but it was not enough, so I borrowed from a friend a large sum to pay for an orthopedic surgeon who had studied in the U.S. He saved my leg, but I was left penniless.

Justice/Injustice

Sick of living in the city, I sold my unfinished house and took my children and my grandmother far away to rebuild a more peaceful life.

Those of you my age will remember, on the road going to Bien Hoa, Long Khanh, just a little past the Hang Xanh Junction, there was the Bien Hoa Bridge. Just a few hundred meters off the bridge, on the righthand side, there was a patch of land near Cat Lai Junction, parallel to a large canal. On that piece of land, there was a row of houses built of light materials. Next to them were huts set up to sell drinks to passersby, and a place to hang out for couples. This land was compensation the government gave to the people when the highway was built. The rest of the land was kept for future lane widening. But since the U.S. aid money had been cut, the construction was suspended indefinitely. As said above, wounded soldiers were out of control and making trouble everywhere. They occupied all the vacant state land and built shabby houses. The war reached its peak, so the government had to turn a blind eye and legalize their home addresses and family declarations. They could sell it if they chose to leave.

In the search for a new place for my family, I found a piece of vacant land. It was ideal as there was a water line leading in from the canal. Across the canal was a rice field, perfect for livestock. Moreover, the owner was eager to sell. I did more research and found out that the piece of land belonged to a major who illegally occupied that land as those wounded soldiers did. He then gave it to his mistress to sell for a profit, not to live in. After we agreed on a price, I went to the commune to get the official transfer papers. My family was given an address and a family declaration. My address was No. 18, An Dien Hamlet, An Phu Commune, Thu Duc District.

I tried to forget the pains of life and rejoice in the fact that my family had a peaceful and idyllic place to live. Although electricity and water were scarcer than in the city, I told myself we would get used to it. I hired people to dig wells and create ponds to raise fish in, and bought materials to build houses and a pig farm. When the house was ready enough to shelter us from the elements, I brought my grandmother and five children there to live. All of us happily accepted the new life, but it was not long before an unforeseeable disaster struck.

One day I was watching the workers build the pigsty when the owner of the neighboring land came over. He was wearing a captain's uniform, the same kind soldiers wore to claim lands like these. He did not live there but had a shack large enough to legalize his claim. With a fierce expression, he informed me that my land belonged to him, and I had unrightfully seized it while he was away. He gave me three days to remove the house and leave, or else I would have to face the consequences. I tried to explain and present the papers proving my legal ownership, not illegal seizure. With a stone-cold expression and not one look at the papers, he told me that anything from the village officials was meaningless. He was the law of the land.

After he left, I tried to reassure my grandmother and the children, believing that we had done nothing wrong. Three days later, right on time, while my family was having breakfast, a large group of police from the district and province arrived to pull down the house and the unfinished pigsty. They put barbed wire around to trap us. The truss fell down on my grandmother's head, making it bleed. My son, in his panic, tripped and fell on the barbed wire, cutting his legs open. I was speechless because I still could not believe what had just happened.

The perpetrators then talked and laughed like it was something trivial. Before leaving, they threatened us that if they came back and my family was still there, they would take stronger measures. I cleaned things up as best I could and ran to the commune to report. The second lieutenant of the commune police was surprised about what the district and the province had done without his authorization. He came to my house to see the damage and make an official report. Then he called the district to let them know that I had done everything according to the legal procedures certified by him, and that the captain could not change anything. Since our house was no longer intact, I sent my children and grandmother back to stay with my mother. I stayed in the ruins because all I had was on the land.

When he learned that the second lieutenant was on

my side, the captain devised a more brutal method. About a week later, at around eight o'clock at night, I was sitting alone in a temporary shack I had built alone with my own hands, since the workers in the neighborhood were too afraid of the captain to help me. I turned the oil lamp as low as possible to save fuel when suddenly I heard the footsteps of people hurrying into my temporary shelter. Before I could react, I was surrounded. One of them pushed me onto a chair, pulled my arms behind me, and tied them up. Then from out of the darkness came the captain, his gun pointed at my head. At that moment, the image of my children, my grandmother, and my mother flashed before my eyes, and tears flowed because I genuinely believed that I would die.

Suddenly, the captain pulled out a piece of paper and a pen from his pocket. He told me that the humanity in him felt for my young children. Otherwise, he would have me shot and thrown my body in the canal and no one would know. I knew it was true because the houses were far away from one another. He demanded that in three days I move out or else be found guilty in the face of the law. I knew it was nonsense, but the "logic" of the one with power made sense, and my family needed me to live. Once I recovered from my panic, I softened my voice and thanked the captain for his mercy, using what was left of my wits to write some squiggly lines and sign the paper. The captain read it, smiled, put it in his pocket, praised me for my obedience, and took his leave.

For the next few days, I tried to rearrange my things

to stay calm, but I was anxious as to what would happen when the date came, but I did not leave! One thing I knew for sure was that I would fight to the end for my family. Never had I felt so alone. Suddenly, I remembered the lieutenant who helped me and went looking for him. When I told him what happened, he was outraged by the captain's abusive actions. He told me to stay put to see what the captain would do if I did not move out and make a clear report of what happened to me for him to submit to higher authorities. Meanwhile, he would send staff on patrol to protect me at night. For the first time in my life, I had met a police officer who fulfilled his duty. I was beyond touched and grateful.

After three days, the captain returned but did not stop by my house. He went around the neighborhood to announce that he would bring me to court and that he would win, and that on the next New Year's Eve, he would level my house and celebrate Tet there. And he extended his invitation to all the neighbors. A few days later, I received a subpoena for the illegal seizure of land. I informed the lieutenant. He reassured me and told me to simply tell the truth, and he would go to court to testify for me if necessary.

On the day of trial, I was shocked to see the captain and his two defense lawyers, dressed in smart black suits. The captain himself wore his military uniform, while I wore my Ao Ba Ba and a Non-La. Initially, the two lawyers took turns presenting the case against me, and then they presented evidence to prove the captain's ownership of the land. In the end, they asked the court to find me guilty of illegal seizure and to rule that I must move right away as per my written agreement and turn over the land to the captain.

When it was my turn, the judge took off his glasses as if to observe me better. He asked if I had written that agreement. I confirmed and asked to defend myself. Once I presented my family declaration and the transfer papers with the commune's certification, I restated that I had never agreed with the captain about his ownership of my land. The reason I had to write the agreement was only to protect my life. But if read carefully, the agreement itself confirmed that I was the owner and that the captain did not object, so it was my right to move out or not move out, regardless of the captain. I had written the following: "My name is . . . owner of Thao Dien farm, No. 18, An Dien Hamlet, An Phu Commune, Thu Duc District. I promise to move out on . . . If I fail to keep my word, I will be punished in the face of the law." The judge looked at me with a smile and asked if I had anything more to say. I simply said that I just wanted to live in peace with my children and grandmother.

Without hesitation, the judge issued a very fair and educational ruling. The land plots in that area were state-owned. In the face of the current situation, the government had granted the people the right to use it until the state needed the use of the land. If that happened, people would be compensated for vacating the land. When the local authorities issued the family declaration and address, possession of the land was determined. The best course of action was to comply with the law: each resides in their house, and the captain was not to trespass on my house or land in any way. The court confiscated the so-called contract to save him from document forgery.

"Go back," the judge turned and told me. "Raise your children into good citizens."

I thanked him, then walked out of the court with tears in my eyes. The belief that justice had prevailed filled my heart. In my ears, the quarrel between the captain and his two lawyers resounded loudly. I hurried off without daring to look back. One thing that did not sit right with me for a long time was that despite my claim that the captain threatened me with a gun, the judge did not seem to consider it worth his consideration. Was he also afraid of the captain's power, or had it become commonplace that army men bullied the people everywhere and the courts were powerless against it?

Police Chief

Once I left the courthouse, I went straight to the An Phu Commune police station. The second lieutenant was beyond glad to hear my good news. In the following days, he often visited my family, exchanging small talk. He wanted to know why I chose to live so far away from the city. I told him about my stance towards the government; what I witnessed had made me lose faith in the people in charge. Out here, I thought I was finally at peace, but it turned out the captain incident happened. I told him truthfully that I did not like the police for their tendency to bully people, but I was lucky to meet him. Otherwise, I could not be sure if I would survive.

One afternoon, he visited me before going to the station as usual. I turned on the radio to listen to the news, and they had a program called: *Born North, Die South*. The program reported the number of North Vietnamese soldiers killed in battle. I told him how saddened I was. When would the North and South stop killing each other?

During the day, I would watch the trucks carrying soldier's bodies pass by my house towards the Bien Hoa Cemetery. At night, I would hear news of soldiers from the opposite side dying in action. I prayed for the war to end, for my nation to be whole again, and for brothers to stop killing each other. The second lieutenant looked at me for a while. He said he understood how I felt, but I must realize prayers and words alone were not enough; only action would work. He asked me if I would join hands if given a chance. I said yes, despite not being sure what I would be asked to do. A few minutes later, he stood up to leave for his patrol. He put a hand on my shoulder.

"You said I'm different from other policemen you've met," he said, voice solemn. "But do you know why?"

"No, sir," I replied.

"Because I am a member of the Southern Liberation Front. Think this over, and I'll stop by tomorrow." Then he left on his motorbike. I stood rooted to the ground, unable to believe my own ears.

That was how I became part of the National Liberation Front. Despite not knowing what exactly I would do, I believed that something that big required many smaller acts. This was the first time in my life I understood what patriotism meant. I felt grief for the fallen Northern soldiers as well as the Southern. In my eyes, when the gunshots ceased and the uniforms were discarded, all those naked bodies were the same— Vietnamese. Their spilled blood would seep into the Viet soil. How heartbreaking. Why would my country from North to South end up in two pieces? Why did foreigners' interference make brothers slaughter each other? They only did so for their own advantage, with no compassion for my compatriots. They had caused parents, children, brothers, husbands, and wives to

separate, one up North and the other down South. This
suffering had gone on too long; it must come to an end.

In the following days, when he had free time, the
second lieutenant taught me how to give injections. I
was terrified of tendon injections, but he was brave
enough to let me practice on him. I also learned how to
bandage wounds. He said he was not sure if it'd come
in handy, but it was good to know just in case.
Everything went well. He said I was smart and had
picked it up quickly, but he did not yet assign me any
task.

One day the second lieutenant came to my house at
noon with a grim face. He told me that because he had
reported my matter to Thu Duc District, the captain's
bullying was no longer tolerated by the district. In
retaliation, the captain ran to the governor and as a
result, the second lieutenant was to be transferred
immediately, in three days. His new place was too far
from his home, which was a massive inconvenience for
him as he had ten young children. I was very distressed
because I understood that because the captain could not
do anything to me, he had turned against the second
lieutenant My savior was in trouble, and I did not know
what to do to help.

Snapping out of my haze, I realized my mother had
a friend whom I called uncle. He was a major in the
army but currently worked at the city hall. I was not
quite sure if he had any authority per se, but at least he
could advise me how I could help the second lieutenant.
After I explained everything, he told me off for letting

matters go this far before letting him know. If he had known, no one would have been able to bully me. Upon hearing that, I was glad. I knew he was willing to help. He told me to sit down while he gathered the facts. He picked up the phone and immediately called the governor. I could only hear this conversation one way, but these were the words of my uncle the major.

"Hey man, you know about the ruckus down on the highway where the Thao Dien shop is, right?"

"You sly dog, that's my niece."

"She didn't tell me, but had I known, you wouldn't have dared touch my niece, would you?"

"Do not play dirty, keep it classy. She is poor, that is why she ended up there with a bunch of kids. Don't you feel guilty?"

"And why did you transfer the second lieutenant? Just let him be."

"Oh no, you're fast! Did he cough up heftily?"

"Jeez, I have already told you. My niece is too poor to even afford a lawyer, but she has got a good head. The captain was rich but dumb as a stump. He hired some lousy lawyers to acquire state property and ended up losing. That is why he is going mad."

"Also, the captain over at Information Communication, why is he so rich? You accepted his money without checking the source. Well that is a recipe for disaster. Now, what do you want to do about the second lieutenant?

"Yeah, that's okay, that place is better, I agree."

"Alright, let us shake on that. Thank you. I owe you one. Drop by my house for a drink whenever."

After hanging up the phone, the major said that the transfer order had already been completed. The governor could not change it, but since he had received the captain's money, he needed to take the second lieutenant elsewhere. Now due to his influence, the second lieutenant would be transferred to Tan Binh District, a much better place. The second lieutenant accepted the transfer with joy.

Old Classmate

O ver the next few days, I tried to settle down by making full use of the land that I was legally entitled to use, digging fishponds, and raising pigs and chickens. I poured all my money into livestock, so I needed another source of income to make ends meet while waiting for the harvest. From the slope of the bridge down to my farm, every house had set up refreshment shops out front. The canal overlooking the field also made for quite a charming scene. I decided to do the same to help with groceries and school supplies for my kids. But if I wanted to make a living this way, I needed to have a small amount of money to kickstart it. Even with wholesale soft drinks, they only delivered orders of at least ten crates. Plus, I needed a few tables and chairs for guests. To be honest, the cost was not much, but I was struggling at the time.

One day, I visited an old classmate. We had known each other since the first day of seventh grade, at Gia Long High School (now Nguyen Thi Minh Khai). During my school days, I was very close to her because we both lost our fathers at a young age. She told me her family was poor, and sometimes she could not afford iced drinks when it was hot. She was quite a beauty, but despite her friendly personality, not many classmates wanted to hang around with her. I could not understand why. But I on the other hand, decided to be her friend because I felt bad about her loneliness.

Later, once we were both grown up and busy with our own lives, we saw each other less. But whenever I happened to go to town, I always paid her a visit. One day as usual, I was passing by her house. I stopped by to check on her well-being, and the change in her house surprised me. As if she was reading the questions written on my bewildered face, my friend joyfully pulled me down onto the brand-new sofa and called the maid to bring us drinks. Then she happily explained to me that she was currently working as an interpreter for MACV (Military Assistant Command Vietnam). The salary was high, but it was nowhere near being a pawnbroker and tontine host. She had just gotten a car to drive to work. Her hands were covered in blinding, sparkling diamond rings. I was both happy and worried.

"So, being a pawnbroker and tontine host," I asked, "aren't you afraid of people coming for you?"

She smiled and patted me on the shoulder, face confident.

"Don't worry, I have protection."

"What do you mean? I do not understand," I quickly asked.

"It's a long story. Stop by another day when you have time and I'll give you the scoop," she giggled.

In the end, I asked her if I could borrow some money to open my shop. I promised to return it after a month. My friend happily gave it to me.

"Don't worry," she said. "Give it back when you are

ready. My line of work makes millions, not some loose change like this."

I thanked her and went on my way. Inside, I was both happy and confused. Even more confusing was when I saw a military jeep with an antenna parked in front of her house. Inside the car was a young soldier sitting as if he was waiting to follow orders. I wondered if a big shot had come to her house that I was not supposed to be seeing. Her husband was a newly enlisted engineer; this soldier could not be him and the jeep could not be his. In the end, as was my nature, I decided that I did not need to know about what was not my business.

Exactly a month later, she came over to my house to get her money back. I had not sold enough soft drinks this month, so I decided to give her all the money I had on hand, and promised to pay it off when I had enough. She refused the money, saying she did not want to be paid in installments. She gave me another week to pay in full because she needed the money to do business. When she left, I called a few shops next door to resell the soft drinks for cheap, gathering money to pay her back everything.

Just a week later, when I was serving drinks for guests, a jeep parked in front of the gate. Then a man in a military uniform stepped into my house. I did not recognize who he was at first. Suddenly, the captain incident came to my mind, and my whole body trembled. What will happen to me now? Which big shot is this one?

When he got closer, the man looked at me and smiled

brightly There was a gentle vibe around him, so it made me less afraid.

"Hello," he said. "The lady asked me to give this piece of paper to you."

I took the piece of paper in a daze, not understanding what it was. After reading it, I realized that this man was here to collect money for my friend. I gave him the money, but before he walked away, he turned to me.

"Give me a bottle of coke. How much is it?"

"Sir, consider it on the house. It is a hot day, and you had to go to all the trouble to come here to collect the money that I had planned to bring over in a few days."

"It is okay. I only do what I am told," he said. "Take the money and keep the change." He paid for his drink and let me keep the change, and then he drove away. I still had no idea who he was, but I recognized that the jeep had an antenna like the one I saw at my friend's house.

One day, when I had the opportunity to go to Ben Thanh Market, I bought some fruit and brought it to her house as a thank-you gift. She happened to have a day off, so she was happy to see me, as she had many things to show and tell me. At this time in her life, she had a large circle of friends. Some were pawnbrokers, some were at her dance club, some she went shopping with, etc. But I was the only friend who had always been with her since day one. And even now, though she was living her rags-to-riches life and I was still wearing rags, I had never been jealous nor judgmental of her.

That day she told me about her love affair with the

general, and showed me the sappy love letters, or rather poems ,that he had written to his lover. I sat there in silence. I disagreed with her actions, but I had no right to object. I asked her what his achievements were that had enabled him to become a general. She told me frankly that he had not fought any battles. In fact, he was elected because he was a Southerner, and was lenient to a fault. There was no risk of him creating a riot, so he was appointed to that position. Every time he heard a gunshot, he would be terrified about which side was winning or losing, not sure which side to be on to save his life.

Finally, before leaving, I turned to my friend.

"If your husband finds out," I said softly in her ear, "you will be in big trouble. What about the kids?"

My friend laughed and pinched the skin on my cheek.

"Do not worry. Everybody knows. Only you just found this out. We are both doing it."

"What do you mean?" I asked in confusion.

"Isn't it obvious? she asked. "If he can play his 'mahjong,' then I can play with my general."

I struggled on, trying my best to adapt to this life. I put all my effort into developing my farm. I did not have the opportunity to see my friend again in the following days, or to be more precise, our worldviews differed in too many ways. Still, I prayed for her peace.

New Friend

A few hundred yards from my farm lived an extremely poor family. Aunt Hai had three children—two older boys, and a young daughter. The eldest was ten years old, then eight years old, and six years old, respectively. Her family lived in a hut made of everything she could gather, like burlap and nylon, with a rusted tin roof. I heard that she came up from Ca Mau (at the end of the South) after her husband's passing. She took her children here for a new life.

Someone hired her to watch over their land without pay, but allowed her to build a hut for her family. She worked odd jobs to make ends meet. Knowing her situation, and also because I needed help to take care of the farm, I hired her family to help me. Since then, we have lived together as a big, happy family. Once, Auntie's eldest son, Thai, was hit by a car and had to go to the hospital. I stayed in the hospital to nurse him until Thai was discharged. In exchange, Auntie stayed at home to take care of the farm. Hung, her second son, was remarkably close to my children. They idolized Hung's skill for catching fish and catching field mice. Hung also gave me a hand when the pigs gave birth.

A memory that I will never forget was when I had free time, I often went to Auntie's hut to relax on the hammock or lay down with her on a wooden bed made of scrap wood she collected somewhere. Auntie and I often talked about the injustices of society. Sometimes we laughed at our own absurdities. One day, Hung caught a bunch of small fish the size of his fingers. Auntie was braising them in a clay pot over a straw fire and when I walked in, the aroma hit my nose.

"What are you cooking? Smells so good," I said.

"Do you want some?" she asked.

"Is there enough?" I asked.

"Goodness, it's just you, me, and the children! We'll make it be enough."

Then she turned to her daughter. "Honey, go to the cupboard and get the most intact bowl for Miss Mai. Hung, and then go to the field and pick some yellow wild vegetable to eat with the stew."

This kind of sentiment had been deeply ingrained in my heart, and was something impossible for me to find in a foreign country. I cherish it like a treasure. Sometimes I love to relive the meaningful days of neighborliness between me and Auntie's family.

Because of his new position and the distance, the second lieutenant did not come to see me as often as before. And before I had received any work related to the revolution, the Liberation Front of the South had already arrived and the war was over. We had lost contact since then. I heard that he was originally from Tien Giang so after the war, he might have returned to his hometown. About a week prior, gunfire and the rumors of the government falling had drawn near, so I

put the farm in Auntie's hands and brought my children
and grandma back to town to stay with my mother.

April 30, 1975

As the news of the Liberation Army drawing closer grew, the more excited I became. The city was in chaos. My mother's house was next to Bach Dang Wharf. I had the chance to leave the country, but I decided to stay. My thoughts were that I did not want to leave my own country, and I also wanted to meet my uncle who would return from the North. I wanted to get to know him and to learn about the death of my father.

Radio news programs were urgent, but I paid them no attention. People were rushing up and down the streets. Women told each other to cut their fingernails short and clean off any nail polish, or else the communists would catch them and pull off their nails with pliers. Young men who were rejected by young girls' families for whatever reasons now got blessings to get married right away, even without a wedding, just two families together. That was how my younger brother got married. Rumor had it that the Communists would force unmarried girls to wed wounded soldiers, especially those who suffered from strange diseases from staying in the jungle for too long.

The chaos unfolded in a magnitude beyond words. Some people ran away, others looted. Motorbikes littered the streets with keys still in the ignition. Men ran up and down the streets in their undershorts. They were Republican soldiers who had shed their uniforms to find an escape. Their leaders were long gone. They were left horrified. People from all walks of life appeared on the street out of nowhere with red scarves on their arms. People said it was the Liberation Front of the South, not the Communists of the North. At that time, I did not understand at all. It just made me uneasy that the difference might mean more fighting and bloodshed. But a few days later, it became clear that the North had prevailed, and history was turning to a new page.

Helping My Compatriots

After the situation quieted down, I brought my grandmother and children back to my Thao Dien farm. When I arrived, I was greeted with something so horrible it rooted me to the ground: my farm had been destroyed. Auntie had hidden a pig away for me. She handed over the pig with tears in her eyes.

"Miss, I tried my best but could not save anything. They were too vicious. I was terrified," she whispered.

I patted Auntie's shoulder, whether to comfort her or comfort myself I was not sure.

"Don't be sad," I said, "we will build it back. The war is over, we will build it back."

Once again, I began with nothing. I told myself I must survive. One important thing was that when I entered the house, something else shocked me: a family of seven—husband, wife, and five children, were occupying my house. I did not know who they were. When asked, the man said he was the son of the nearby An Phu Temple keeper. He had served as an auxiliary to American commandos in the field, and his name was Duc. His father did not let him stay in the temple for fear of his political involvement. Without a proper place to live, he decided to stay at my house without my permission.

Seeing his hardship, I let him stay at the far end of my

land and told him to build a house for his family. He insisted on staying in my house, as he did not have money to buy materials for a new house. Feeling sorry for him, I gave him some money to buy enough wood and palm leaves for a small house. After building the house, he said just shelter was not enough. He needed something to feed his wife and children, something like my fishpond. Once again, I sympathized and let him dig a pond next to my two others. The day I released fish into my ponds, I also gave him a few hundred. I had to remind him that his pond was blocking the water flow in and out of my ponds, so if he was not careful and blocked the flow, my fish would die. He assured me that he understood, which somewhat reassured me.

One more important thing I learned was that Auntie's husband, who served in the revolution army, had died in action. Her family was certified as a family with meritorious services to the revolution. I was happy for her, thinking her life from here on would be better. However, the reality was that the country was unstable. Everyone was in the same boat of poverty, except those who had lost their way and lost their ideals. Auntie did not complain nor blame anyone. She just continued as if nothing had changed and patiently waited. I love and respect her very much.

At that time, the government needed to be set up, but there was not enough workforce. After a few meetings, the people in the hamlet elected me to be the Head of the Women's Affairs Committee. This position was unpaid, so no one wanted to accept it. But for me, this was the time for everyone to lend our nation a helping hand. Opposite my house was the Press Village, where the Republican officials went to re-education camps. Their wives had free time, so I asked them to help me because there was a heavy workload.

The Personnel Committee consisted of myself as president, a vice president, secretary, social affairs officer, and finance officer. Aside from holding meetings to implement the government's policy, every day we were tasked with receiving bread, fish, meat, and vegetable rations to sell to everyone at the price decreed by the government. I also visited the families who needed the most help, especially mothers who were too malnourished to feed their children. At the same time, I raised awareness of birth control. Some farmers were angry with me about this issue, thinking that it was a private matter, and that the state had no right to instruct about this topic. In the evening, I organized classes for the illiterate. I worked tirelessly. Others on the committee would often find excuses not to attend, but for me, this was an opportunity to help my people and serve my country in need.

One day, the committee vice president requested a board meeting with everyone. She made quite a shocking proposal. Usually every morning, the finance director and I would go to the cooperative to get bread and bring it back for retailing at the official price. Each person was allowed to buy one loaf. At times, when there were leftover loaves because some people could not afford it, the finance director would go out on her bike to inform people who wanted more. We had to sell all the bread in time to get fresh food to sell for lunch.

Now the vice president wanted us to hold off on the bread and only sell a few for show. The rest, if smuggled across the bridge, someone would buy at the underground price. In her opinion, we had no reason to work without pay, to which the committee secretary and social affairs director agreed. I strongly objected as it went against my conscience. Sometimes I would even pay out of my own pocket for the poor, so why would I do something like that? At first, the finance director was hesitant, opting for whatever the majority chose. But in the end, she sided with me.

I thought everything was resolved but a week later, the hamlet board of directors called me up as I had been reported for cheating and falsely weighing. Shocked and confused, I asked to find the underlying cause of the matter. The accusers said that the weight of the fish and shrimp I had sold them was false—that I had weighed the fish and charged for 100 grams, but it was only 90 grams when they weighed it at home. I tried to defend myself, saying that I would never cheat. They refused to listen. They accused me of hypocrisy, taking advantage of my position to make money.

"Now we know why you worked so passionately even with no pay," they shouted.

I was numb with pain. Words choked in my throat. In the end, the hamlet people demanded that the board let me go, as my trustworthiness was compromised. While the board was still making the decision, the vice president, secretary, and social affairs director, suggested that they could take over my position instead of finding someone new. It dawned on me then why I was wrongly accused.

The next morning, the board of directors had yet to decide, so I still went to the market to pick up the seafood. I requested a meeting with the hamlet people and the board before I distributed the fish and shrimp. Everyone gathered around me like in a trial. I asked a resident to weigh the shrimp while everyone waited. Around fifteen minutes later, I asked another resident to weigh the same portion of shrimp. Of course, the weight had declined because the water on the shrimp had drained off, right then and there, so of course some time later, when the shrimp was taken home and weighed again on a home scale, it would have weighed even less.

Having cleared my name, I walked over to the representative to submit my resignation, ignoring the murmur of the bustling crowd. I hurried out of the meeting room in tears as I heard someone call out to me.

"We understand, please don't resign."

Even though my resignation was final, I still served the people when they needed me, like when they were sick or gave birth, and when their pigs needed vaccinations or stopped eating.

I remembered once my neighbor Uncle Nam kicked an old coconut tree with his bare foot and a splinter got stuck deep in his toe. Having heard of my skill, he asked me to help get the splinter out. I referred him to the clinic, but he insisted on me because he heard I had a good hand that could cure anything. I agreed to help him on the condition that he would not yell even if it hurt. If he yelled, I would run away because I had to use a surgical knife to remove the splinter. I did not know if it was thanks to my good skill or his good immunity, but it did not take long for me to nurse the wound until it healed.

In return for my help, he gave me a bunch of ripe bananas.

"Try one, it's very sweet," he told me.

I grabbed one and took a small bite, saving the rest for my kids and grandma. The banana was sweet, as sweet as neighborly love.

Another time, in the middle of the night, Mr. Bay, a farmer, carried a lamp over and asked for my help with his wife who was in labor. His house was too deep in a field; they would not make it to the clinic in time. I yelled at him that I was not a midwife so how would I know how to deliver a baby?

"You're not a midwife," he said in a hurry, "but you have given birth, so you must have experience. Moreover, we know you are a kind person. We trust you can handle it."

I followed him, praying hard. Entering the house, I immediately told him to boil some water. After all the sanitary procedures, I summoned up all my courage and helped Mrs. Bay give birth to a beautiful son. With all my composure, I finished the job of a midwife. Before leaving for my home, I told Mr. Bay to take his wife to the clinic the next day to check if there was any bit of the placenta remaining. I was not professional, so I was afraid there was still a risk of retained placenta.

Stepping out of his house, my legs suddenly trembled. I broke out in sweat, unable to comprehend what I had just done. Two days later, I went to visit the family and learned that Mrs. Bay did not go to the clinic because she believed she was safe with me and everything would be fine. Mr. and Mrs. Bay named the boy Hen (Good Luck).

My Uncle

Since the day of reunification, I had always been looking out for news of my uncle in the North. A lot of people who enlisted in the North had returned to the South, but why hadn't I heard anything from him—could he have fallen in action? I had previously hoped that one day I would meet him, and would ask him about my father and learn what he did. In fear, I waited.

God makes things happen for me. One muggy day, I was at home looking out when my uncle walked in. I could not remember his face because I was too young on the day he left, but my instincts told me that person was my uncle.

"Uncle," I cried.

"I'm here," he replied softly.

I ran into his embrace, crying like a baby, unable to stop the sobs spilling out of my throat. My uncle's cheeks were wet with tears. That day he stayed to have dinner with my family and told us about his older brother. He missed him dearly and was always proud of him. Thanks to my father, my uncle became a useful member of society. He used to be a drunkard when he was young. One day, during that painful time for our country, my father looked at him, eyes filled with sorrow.

"The country is falling apart because of your behavior. If all youngsters were like you, then who would help this country in the face of adversity?"

My father's words shook him to the core. He joined the revolution with my father, but when my father was captured by the French, he sent a messenger to warn my uncle to retreat deep in the jungle, so my uncle ran away to the North. Once he made it to the North, the news of my father's death also reached him.

I asked him how he knew of my mom's house and was able to find me there, to which he only smiled, saying there was nothing unknown to him. He even knew about my brother's death back in the Year of the Monkey. I asked him about my great aunt's child, to which he sadly replied that he died in action. My poor great auntie had only one child. She had patiently waited years and years for the day they would reunite. The sheer disappointment took her life not long after.

I did not dare ask him about his job, but I knew that he was stationed at the police training school for the old regime. Every day on his way to work, he would pass by my house, sometimes stopping by to give my children a bag of sugar or a bunch of bananas. I once went to visit his house. His address was three-turn deep in a small alley, a rundown house of about sixteen square meters with a uniform raincoat stretched on the ceiling to prevent leakage. At the back there was a kitchen covered with metal sheets and rickety planks. I asked why most of the cadres were given large luxury houses, but he lived here. His reply was full of jest.

"The deeper you go, the quieter the house. The smaller the house, the warmer it is."

Challenging Time

It was a financially tough time for everyone. I had to bend over backwards to make ends meet for the family, or should I say two families because whatever I earned, I shared half with Mr. Duc's family. I explained to my children that others need food just like we do. We share our food and God will grant us something else.

During my business travels, the biggest obstacle was to deal with tax collection checkpoints. The government did not prepare to win the South that fast, so the result was they had to use the staff from the office of the old regime. They grossly abused their power, exploiting traders. The drivers who had been trading on that road before the day of reunification knew their faces well and even their names. There was a time when I went to buy coal in Central Vietnam to bring it back and sell to the cooperative. Due to my lack of experience, I did not pack my load tight enough, so the number of bags was less than the tonnage. When I declared to pay tax, the tax was counted according to the size of the truck. I tried to explain but they did not listen, telling me that only by unloading it all for a recount would I convince them. They knew it was impossible for me. That was why they imposed such a condition.

The tax required by the stationmaster at the

checkpoint was of no fixed price—arbitrary, and without a receipt. About half a kilometer away, there were others in plain clothes armed with guns, red cloths tied around their arms, asking for taxes again. If you couldn't afford the tax, then you traded whatever you had for whatever the stationmaster needed.

There were times I was caught in the rain and had to shelter in the forest for a few days before coming back to the cooperative. I had sold only enough coal to buy a basket of potatoes and a few kilos of dried fish. Even then, I always gave half of it to Mr. Duc.

As life got tougher, I had to send my two older children to live with my mother in Saigon to help support the family. At 5:00 a.m., they sold firewood to street cafes that sprouted up everywhere, then returned to sell salt at the morning market. At noon, they sold iced tea to vendors on the street. Everyone was struggling to stay afloat.

The Press Village was an upscale neighborhood, about a kilometer from the main road. I did not understand the name, but as far as I knew, most of the homeowners were high-ranking officers in the Republic army. On the way to the neighborhood, past a public swimming pool, on the righthand side there was a turn. At the end, there was a luxury villa with three floors and a terrace, located on a large plot of land with a spacious garden. This was the home of a former lieutenant colonel who was away for re-education schooling. I could not recall which branch he belonged to, armor or artillery, but certainly not infantry. The rest of the family consisted of his wife, the mother-in-law who could not walk normally due to a stroke, the daughter with two children but no husband in sight, the teenage son, and a niece who also served as their housekeeper. The reason I knew of this family was because I was the head of the Women's Affairs Committee. In the initial stages, I held a lot of press conferences to implement the government's guidelines and policies, so the wife, as the head of the household, contacted me regularly at meetings. Her name was Ms. Kham.

I did not understand why she was very fond of me and often helped me out by sending me to sell her household things. For example, she set the price of the item, and I would bring it to the market to sell. If I sold it for a higher price, the surplus would be my share. There is one thing that I still cannot understand even now about the state of our country at the time. Many people had to sell everything they owned in their house: dishes, wardrobes, tables, chairs, and clothes to buy food. On the contrary, there were also many buyers. So, who were the rich ones? I had to bend over backwards just to earn enough to feed my family, but I had heard that there were also people who had lots of money. It was confusing.

One day, Ms. Kham called me over to her house to prepare clothes to sell. She trusted me enough now to allow me in her room of precious belongings.

"In the past, before the war ended, every time my husband came back from the war, I couldn't count all the money he brought back," she said proudly.

I suddenly asked a silly question.

"What did he buy and trade for so much money?"

"Sell, not buy. Sold everything."

She went quiet and I dared not ask more questions. Then she changed the topic.

At that time, trading was quite interesting. The government prohibited trading on the street, but whoever had a bit of capital gathered in a certain place at a small market. Sometimes public officials came to chase them away but after a while, officials started to collect "ground rent" for the spot. It seemed like everyone worked together to get by.

As for me, with no capital or possessions, I only sold what Ms. Kham wanted to sell. I had to carry everything and because I had no place to sit when selling clothes, I had to wear them all. If anyone wanted to buy something, I would take everything off, layer by layer. Ms. Kham was heftier than me, so the shirts fit fine, but the pants were a nightmare. I had to safety-pin them on around me like a clown in a circus.

Once, Ms. Kham registered to raise pigs for the cooperative. She also raised one more pig for herself. On the day of the slaughter, she called me over to help sell it. I was reluctant, unsure how to do it. If I carried the meat in baskets, I would get caught by the police and the entire thing would be confiscated. Raising pigs outside the cooperative with the government was illegal. How would I pay her back then?

In fact, she had a lot of smart ideas. She divided the meat into half a kilo parcels, put them in plastic bags, then wrapped them around my stomach. Outside, I wore a big top that made me look like I was pregnant. That is how I went to the market. I sold fresh meat by lifting my shirt to show off my fake belly and someone would buy a parcel of meat right away.

That day, I sold out all the meat in a flash. Instead of walking back, I rewarded myself by taking an auto-rickshaw ride. As soon as I sat down, the passengers next to me tried to move away from me and looked at me in distaste. I followed the gaze of the woman opposite myself when I realized that my shirt was stained with pig's blood.

"It's pig's blood," I blurted out in exasperation, "Can't you smell the pig stench?"

Suddenly, everyone laughed sympathetically. They were also traders like me, each in their own way. I laughed along, eyes stinging, due to the sweat, dust, or tears.

Hard as it was, I always told myself if others could survive then so could I. Just endure until the country becomes stable, then everything would be better. But one day, the police summoned me to their headquarters for some reason I completely did not understand. The security officer told me that someone accused me of colluding with the puppet state officials who would often meet at my house at night. How else could my family afford to eat white rice? I was terrified because if I were arrested for crimes I did not commit, what would happen to my children? At that time, the whole country had to eat old, moldy rice mixed with corn, barley, and sweet potatoes. We would be fined if we got caught eating plain white rice. I did not know what had happened to the nation's rice crops. Vietnam's main agricultural product was rice for exporting.

"Gentlemen," I said as I trembled, trying to keep my composure. "That is false. On my property there is Mr. Duc, a former American Ranger. If I ever met with anyone, he would be a witness. My house is next to the canal where the soldiers often go fishing. They fish and play with my kids, and sometimes even give them half a cup of sugar or a cup of rice. And Mr. Duc, he comes to my kitchen to check my rice pot every day. He knows I eat rice mixed with roots like everyone else. If you don't believe me, just ask him."

The security men looked at each other. The oldest in the group looked at me for a long time and then told me that it was Mr. Duc who reported the incident to the police. I fell to the ground. I did not understand, nor whether to believe it or not. After that, my house was often visited by the "30th revolutionists." On many sleepless nights worrying about whether I could afford to feed my children, I would lie on a hammock hanging in my front yard, thinking about a solution to make money, when the 30th revolutionists would come in.

"Waiting for someone?" they asked.

"I couldn't sleep, not waiting for anyone."

"Can't sleep due to dissatisfaction with the government, yes?"

"No, sir."

"You better not be."

When my mother came to visit me, I went to report it and asked for permission for the visit. There was a time when we forgot the curfew time and we were about ten minutes late when the 30th revolutionists barged in with guns and asked why my mother was still there, and if we were waiting for someone.

Allow me to explain about the "30th revolutionists." After the unification of the country, some people who had previously worked for the old regime, but were not of high rank, were reused by the state. Others who were previously underrepresented in society, now wanted to receive merit from the state to make profit. They were only good at putting on shows and bullying the people excessively. So we called them "30th revolutionists," meaning they just joined the revolution from April 30, 1975, after reunification.

It was tough, but my family tried to keep our two fishponds populated in the hope that when the fish were sold, we would have some money to save in case of illness. One morning I woke up early to feed the fish and saw that most of them had died and floated to the surface. I ran out to check the pipes but did not see anything unusual. Feeling suspicious, I ran across to Mr. Duc's pond where I saw a bag of grass stuffed in the pipe to prevent water from flowing through into my ponds.

Furious, I called him out.

"Why did you do that?" I asked. He glared at me.

"Did you see me do it?" he shouted back. "Don't make baseless accusations or I'll report you."

Right away, he went to the hamlet committee and reported me for slander. His little kid let it slip that her father caught a lot of fish in my pond at night, so she thought it belonged to her father. I told the committee that I was tired of this, and to settle it however they could. Then I called someone to wholesale the fish. The money was not much as the fish did not have time to mature. Moreover, I sold some and gave some to the neighbors as they were as poor as I was.

After many nights of thinking, I realized that I had tried my best to continue living in my homeland and loving my people, but I could not stand it anymore. My children were growing up with no future because my family contributed nothing to the revolution. What if they could not go to university? I could not survive the new economy. I was chased to a dead end with no other choice. I had to find a way to survive for my family, but how?

The government had a homestay plan called "new economic zones" for families willing to move far away from the cities to undeveloped land. Depending on the size of your family, you would receive acres of land to cultivate and start your new life. It was a good plan, but we had no workforce. With six children, the oldest being just twelve, my grandma, and myself, we would not survive out there.

Escape

In the hamlet, there was a new family who just moved in right after April 1975. I had no idea where they came from. They built a large wooden two-story house on a nice piece of land. It was owned by a hefty couple in their early forties. They had eight children, an elderly mother, two dogs, and the youngest brother in his thirties who was mentally challenged. He lived in a shack in a corner at the end of the land. People called him Seventh Short (in Vietnamese culture, the father is the first). He was the sixth child in his family and compared to his siblings, he was short and chubby.

The wife had a small shop in the market, selling what she bought and buying what people sold. The husband was an interesting man. He was a bicycle racer for the big city. He always kept his bicycle on the second floor where his bedroom was, and once in a while in the early morning, neighbors would hear him yelling and cursing at his wife. He would throw his bicycle from the second floor to the ground because his wife had kept him up late the night before for some enjoyment, so he didn't have enough energy for the race in the morning. I did not know his real name, but people called him Fifth Crowbar. The rumor was that he used to be a gangster when he was young, his weapon was a crowbar, and he was the fourth child in his family.

Right after April 1975, Vietnam went through countless economic hardships: an international embargo, subsidy economy, invading enemies at both ends of the country, floods, droughts, and people falling deep into poverty.

At that time, many people tried to find ways to escape by sea or by land. Their hope was to find another country where they could find opportunities to make a living. A new business deal popped up in secret between owners of transportation, mostly boats, and people who had gold and wanted to escape. Fifth Crowbar was the go-between for connecting those two groups. One time I checked with him about how much I had to pay if I wanted to escape. He looked at me with pity and smiled. Then he lowered his voice and told me not to think about it; there was no hope for me, no way I could come up with that amount of gold. Besides, I had six children, and the youngest was only three years old.

What I found out was that all the transactions are paid in gold. In Vietnamese we call it "cay" (one cay equals .829496 ounces). Each person had to pay from ten to fifteen cays for men, and five to eight cays for women; no children were allowed. I had no cays, and I had children. Looking at my desperate face, he felt sorry for me. He suggested if I could pay him one cay, he would introduce me to a wealthy family. They didn't need gold, but they needed a maid. I had to work for them wherever they settled until I paid off four cays, which I owed them. They were ready to leave.

Fifth Crowbar convinced me that I should accept that

offer, because after I paid off the debt, I would have money to send back to take care of my children. My heart sank down into my stomach with the thought of leaving my children behind. "No, a thousand times no," I said to myself. We would survive or die together; we could not be separated, regardless of our situation.

One day I was on the way home after a citizen meeting. Seventh Short stopped me and asked if I wanted to escape. He had overheard his brother. I was afraid people would find out and report it to the police. I could go to jail. I told him that he must have been mistaken, because since I was so poor, how could I ever dream about something like that?

Suddenly, he took my hand and said,

"I have felt love for you for a long time. If you married me and took me with you, I would show you the boat nobody wants. We would leave with your children, and you wouldn't have to cry."

Knowing about his mental challenges, I knew he would not take a rejection easily, so I told him to keep it a secret and I would think about it. In his family, nobody paid attention to him. They fed him and let him drink leftover beer. He was always around, just for food and drink. He continued to give me his message a few more times, and I decided to find out more details. Apparently, there was a man who operated a barge for the government to transfer materials from Saigon to build Vung Tau Port (about one hundred kilometers away). He had asked Fifth Crowbar to arrange an escape business. He got turned down by Fifth Crowbar because he thought it was a crazy idea and would not work, and that he should forget about it. I decided to meet that man to learn more about the barge.

His name was Tam and he was a navy sailor under the old Republic. The government used him because he knew how to operate a barge, but there was a military guard from the North always with him. The barge was used to carry diesel oil and towed by a big boat, but at that time, an engine was installed by the state on top of the barge, and was run by diesel oil. After a long talk, I understood the situation well enough to plan to escape with him. It was not easy, but in my mind, it was possible.

The barge was a large rectangular metal box. On top at one corner was an engine, and next to it was a round open space with a ladder to go under. At the other corner was an empty shipping container. The escapees would go down the ladder and hide inside the box in a large room. At the end of the room, there was a divided wall about three feet high, three feet wide, and the same length as the barge. Tam's job was to clean that area and fill it with clean water. We would add chlorine so we could drink during our journey. We laid out all the questions and tried to find reasonable answers.

We needed oil, lots of oil, and we could buy it through the illegal market. Tam had no money, and people who had money did not trust him enough to join him so we decided that I would raise the money. I was poor, but my credit was good.

I would buy dried food such as cooked, dehydrated rice, and MREs. During the war, these items were food for military operations. They were left behind when American troops withdrew from Vietnam. With no authority, poor people brought it home. At first, they did not know what to do with it, but then they made a fortune when the rich tried to escape. They needed food that would not spoil. There was no fixed price, only supply and demand.

To secretly transfer food to the barge, I would wrap it around my stomach, wear a loose shirt, and pretend I was Tam's pregnant mistress. I met with him whenever the barge docked, emptied the food, and replaced it with rags around my stomach.

We had to sleep in nylon hammocks because we flooded water about ankle deep into the space where people were going to hide to create some humidity. There was a place to hang them.

We needed a compass, a large one. Tam's cousin had one. We took his family of four adults with us so no gold was exchanged for the compass.

There was a farmer who owned a farm by the river where we got onboard. We would use this location for a gathering permit. Reason: Meeting Co-op raising pigs. His family of five adults would join us with no gold. (At that time, meeting was illegal.)

We could not ask the guard to leave with us. We could not harm him. Coming from the North, he had suffered so much because of the war. In Saigon, he had learned to enjoy girls and drink but his military income was not enough to give him that pleasure. He would steal the diesel oil from the barge, and Tam would sell the oil in an illegal market. We would double the money in case he got discharged or jailed after the government found out we stole the barge. We wanted him to have enough money to start a small business when he got back to civilian life. He thought Tam got a good deal on diesel oil in the black market. He had a habit of staying with girls until the next morning. Then he caught a bus to go back to Vung Tau on time to join Tam, because it took a longer time for the barge to go back. When the time came, we will leave without him.

We agreed on a preliminary plan. Back home, I needed to teach my children to swim. If they could just keep afloat, someone could save them because I did not know how to swim. I asked my oldest son, who was ten, to go to the neighborhood to ask for an old banana plant and cut it in a length of about two feet to be used as a floater. We waited for low tide and they all learned how to float (we lived right by the canal).

My mom's friend was a doctor. His family of nine adults and a three-year-old girl had tried to escape a few times. They lost lots of gold, but did not make it. He was about to give up. I approached him and asked how much gold he had left, and if he still wanted to leave. I also told him my plan. He sadly replied.

"We want to go, but all I have left is ten cays."

I asked, "Do you trust me?"

He responded quickly. "Yes, no doubt."

"Good, you are in," I told him. Go prepare drugs for the children. They need to be sedated so they will not be afraid and cry when we hide."

In the following days, I contacted and invited more people who wanted to leave. In the end, I collected forty-five cays, fifty-three adults, and three toddlers who would join me.

Betrayal

One week before departure, we had the last meeting. Tam told me the total number of adults was seventy. He gave me excuses about the sad circumstances of his relatives and his relatives' relatives. I understood he wanted to make some money for himself. I thought of the people who did not have much but wanted to search for a better life just like me, so I agreed. But greed has no limit. Seventh Short overheard Tam made the deal with Fifth Crowbar to take five Chinese men and leave my family behind. They would collect fifty cays, and split it between themselves. They met at the same bar every night. I located the place and watched them for two nights to know for sure what I needed to know. The third night was a heavy rain night, the road was dark, and the sound of raindrops was loud. I followed Tam walking home by himself. He was drunk like a fish and fell down a couple times. I waited patiently. Then my chance came when he fell into a deep puddle of mud. When he tried to get up, I pushed him down, sat on his stomach, and put my Swiss Army Knife under his chin. I was shaking because I was cold and angry, but my voice was so stern.

"I gave you whatever you asked of me. If you want

to betray me, I will take your life and go to jail. I only scared you this time, but not the second time. You will have to lie when people ask you about the scar."

He cried and asked for forgiveness. I left him with a scar for life on his chin.

But let us be fair to everybody. Now it is my turn to talk about my fairness. In my whole life, there was only one time I used my charm and lied to a man who trusted me with all his heart. Seventh Short was that man. He loved me and wanted to be with me. That was the reason he led me to meet Tam. Right from the beginning, I just wanted to get information out of him, but I was also afraid he might tell the authorities if I rejected his idea. I told him I would send my children away on that barge and I would stay back and marry him. The only intimacy we had so far was holding hands. I said, "Keep everything else until we get married." He believed it. Shame on me!

Three days before departure, the amount of gold left in my hands was five cays. I thought of Seventh Short. I wanted to repay him for his kindness and find comfort in my soul. I gave him the rest of the gold I had. I told him, "Keep this gold for me. When my children are safely out of the country, I will come back, we will get married, and we will use this gold to open a small business together."

He was happy like a child. I gave him a kiss on his forehead and left. That was the last time I saw him. Five years later in America, I had news he married and opened a small shop fixing bicycles. He was no longer living under his brother's wings. He was an independent man, and I am free of guilt.

After I took care of Seventh Short, my children and I went back to stay at my mom's house while waiting for the time. The place where the journey began was close to her house. My neighbors thought my family was going to a " new economic zone." They wondered if we could survive.

When I bid farewell to Auntie Hai, we could not say a word. We just hugged each other and cried, promising that we would try to live so we could meet again one day.

The day I left my homeland, I had only my six children and the clothes on my body. This was the first time in my life that I was away from my grandma. She was the first person to hold me in her arms when I was born. She named me and nurtured me until adulthood. Before my father died, he entrusted us to Grandma to take care of us. When I got married, she helped take care of my children. She was by my side through every up and down of my life. She gave her life for me, but now I had to leave her behind. This decision broke my heart, but I had to let her stay. She had lived her life for me; I could not let her die at sea because of me.

Escaping by sea was full of danger: looting, raping, killing, and storms. Survival was in the hands of fate. On the day of my departure, I said goodbye to my grandma and my mom, but I did not dare to look them in the eye. I did not have the courage.

"Wait for me, I'll come back," I said briefly.

I turned away quickly without looking back because I knew that even a glimpse of them would change my mind.

Two years later, in my absence, my mother passed away. In the year after that, my grandmother followed. To this day, a feeling of loss plagues my heart when I think about grandma and mother. I have not had the opportunity to repay the ones who gave birth to me and nurtured me. I do not know if there is a next life for me to do just that.

Refugee Camp

I do not want to talk too much about our voyage leaving home because compared to others, we were lucky. It took forty-one days for us to reach Pulau Besar, Malaysia. We faced pirates, were short of food and water, got beat up by Thai police, endured storms at night and the burning sun during the day, but we escaped death and safely reached shore. I learned a valuable lesson about world politics and diplomacy on this trip: there were no friends nor enemies, and nothing lasts forever. For example, at one time the nearby country of Thailand stood in line with the Republic of Vietnam, but when the situation changed, they brutally plundered, raped, and killed countless Vietnamese while crossing the sea. They blamed pirates but in fact, we were robbed and beaten by Thai police, and even filmed and photographed before we found refuge.

The second lesson I want to mention here was the selfishness of people of the same blood and on the same boat with me and my six children. My shipmates came from all social classes. Most of them were people with positions, even religious leaders, but they fought for our limited food supplies like animals. Whatever the circumstances, their egos came first. That was the rule on the boat. When we got to the refugee camp, where everyone should share and support those in the same situation, they played the role of the elites, refusing to do anything.

A good example is that while we were staying in a refugee camp in Malaysia, the United Nations High Commissioner provided us with medicine. Some people needed guidance when taking the medicine. Knowing that in the camp there was a doctor who used to be a congressman in the old regime, I asked him for some help just for a few hours a day in dispensing medicine. He refused, claiming that he did not have time. In fact, the challenge for me was that there was too much time in the camp. There was nothing to do besides sitting and waiting for salvation. When my begging proved useless, I went to see the doctor again together with the famous writer Mai Thao. This time the doctor outright said that he was a congressman, and he needed rest to think about how to deal with the U.S. Congress when he arrived in the U.S. He would testify before the Senate and the House of Representatives, so he could not do things that were not worthy of his position.

What was even more shameful when he came to America, was that he published in the Vietnamese daily newspaper, *Tien Phong*, that he had taken care of the refugees in the camp. I immediately posted a rebuttal and challenged him to speak up, but he went silent. He knew that I was telling the truth. I never heard about him after that.

In the camp, there was a pregnant lady at her due date. She confided to me about the anxiety of giving birth in a camp too far from the city. I reassured her that

I would do everything to help her. Then on a moonless night she called for me. We had to wade through knee-deep water to get to the Malaysian police checkpoint. Despite the language barrier, the police understood just by looking at us that she was about to go into labor. He ran away for a while and came back with an elderly woman. Working together, we delivered a baby girl safely. I made a gesture of thanks to the woman who helped me. She smiled and said words that I did not understand. Then she hurried into the darkness to go back home. I suddenly realized that in times of need, some people were willing to help others regardless of language, skin color, and race. On the contrary, some were willing to ignore their own race in dire times. To this day I am grateful to the elderly woman for helping us strangers.

Settling down

After six months of waiting in the camp, my children and I finally reached America. In the early days, I had to face the test of life and its value. We were the only Vietnamese family to settle in that neighborhood. The neighbors knew that I had come to their country with six children empty-handed. They joined hands to help us by donating clothes and household items, new and old. The food given was so much that I had to cook turkey seven diverse ways to change the taste for different meals.

Next, a social worker came and gave me cash, free medical checkups, and food vouchers. She said this was what I would receive every month from the government. I was ecstatic but worried at the same time as I had not made any money.

"How will I be able to pay it back? "I asked her.

"Don't worry. You have six children; the government will take care of you and your children for the rest of your life," she reassured me.

"Where does the government get money for us?" I wondered aloud.

"From the taxes of working people," she replied.

"No, that is not fair. I want to work. Please help me."

"You really do not understand anything, do you?" she said. "If you go to work, you only get the minimum wage, with no health insurance. What if your children get sick?"

It was confusing and embarrassing. When I went to the market, I had to pay with food stamps. I could feel the look of disapproval from other shoppers. Was it true or was it just my conscience telling me that I was a parasite who leeched off others' sweat and tears? I was very judgmental of myself.

A few months later, I took my driver's license test and decided to look for a job. I reported it to the Social Security office and stopped asking for benefits. The staff told me that was ridiculous. They reminded me of my family's health insurance. I laughed and said I would pray for good health. If we got sick, I would pay in installments because U.S. hospitals cure people first and charge money later.

Here is how we started working for wages. First, I applied for a dishwasher job at a restaurant. No one hired me because I looked sickly and could not carry the dishes. I next applied to households that needed cleaning services. That was my chance. Every day I had a job. On weekends, my children and I mowed lawns for the neighbors. Then I found a job as a kitchen assistant at a restaurant. Not long after I became a cashier for a bank, I had full health insurance for all of us.

From the very first day, I instructed my children about one thing: "Study hard, use your labor to bring food to the table; there is no undignified job. You are free to choose employment to support yourself. We left our country to find a better future, not to become beggars in America. I will not forgive you if you do anything to dishonor and shame our race."

Meet Again!

After the whirl of orienting for the future, in addition to learning the culture, settling down, and finding work to raise my children, I also suffered homesickness. I missed home, my town, and craved the sound of my language. Many nights once the children slept, I cried alone. The place where we lived was a small city in the state of Maryland. To meet my compatriots, I went to a shop owned by Vietnamese people that sold Chinese and Thai groceries. This place was about a forty-minute drive from where I lived. At this time, the U.S. and Vietnam had yet to establish diplomatic relations, so Vietnamese goods were unavailable. One day, I ran into my old high school classmate at that store. She lived in Virginia, the state next to Maryland, a one-hour drive away.

There was no greater joy than meeting a Vietnamese person in Maryland, especially an old friend. She invited me to her house so we could visit longer. Besides the joy of the reunion with my classmate, I met with another surprise. A man suddenly came out to greet me from the back of the house.

"Hello. I didn't think I would run into you here," he said. "How great!"

I shyly greeted him back, unable to recall where I had

met him. My friend laughed aloud.

"Aren't you surprised? It's the general, remember?"

"Oh, I remember now. I only met him once when he was wearing a military uniform, so it was a bit different."

This was the same general who once came to my house to collect the money I owed my friend. His military uniform had made me so flustered that I did not dare to look at his face clearly years ago. Later, I often cooked Vietnamese dishes to treat my friend, her husband, and the general. I could not help but think it was the changing circumstances that had allowed me to welcome these men in my house today. Oh well, it was precious enough to be in the company of other Viets when I was a stranger in Maryland.

For quite a long time, about a couple of years, despite our frequent contact through house visits and phone calls, I had never asked about the presence of the general in her house. I had assumed that they must be splitting the rent. Since rental fees in this country were expensive, situations like this were common. One afternoon towards the end of the year, it was quite cold despite the light snowfall. My family was sitting down for dinner when the doorbell rang. I did not run to the door right away, skeptical of who would be coming to my house at this hour. I called to the door in English.

"Excuse me, who is this?"

"It's me."

Surprised by the sound of the Vietnamese language, I immediately opened the door and saw in front of me the familiar figure of a man shivering in the cold. I recognized that it was the general.

"Come inside. It's freezing outside. Where are the others?"

"I'm traveling alone."

His soft, unhappy tone drew my attention. On a closer look, I realized his hat and coat were covered with snow. Perhaps he had been standing outside for a while.

"Give me your coat and hat. The fireplace is over there; go warm yourself up. Then join us for dinner."

I rushed to the kitchen to set a place for him at the table. Passing by the living room, I saw him adding firewood to the furnace. He must have been very cold.

"Make yourself at home and have some dinner. It's nothing much, but the hot soup will warm you up in no time. Eat first, we'll talk later."

Dinner passed in a tense atmosphere. My children did not engage in any conversation, just scarfed down their meal and excused themselves. Everyone was in a rush to find out why he was at my house. Intuition told me that something serious must have happened to him. I just could not tell why he came to find me. After dinner, the children went to the next room to study, leaving me and the general in the living room.

"So, what happened?" I asked. "Does anyone know you're here?"

I asked him this question because I knew full well we were only acquaintances. The times when he came over before, I considered him a guest. Furthermore, he and my friend always hosted parties with loads of people which I never attended as we did not share the same political attitudes. He reluctantly explained.

"I came here because out of all of our many friends, you are the only one I truly respect."

"So, how can I help you?"

He gave no answer, only a sudden sigh. His face was wet with tears. I quickly passed him the tissue box.

"Thank you," he said. "I need your help with something. Only you are capable of this."

In doubt, I responded, "I'm no better than anyone else, but just tell me. I'll try to help you to the best of my ability."

He confided matters that went beyond my imagination. I went from one surprise to another. According to him, he used to be my friend's lover. The husband was aware, but he cared about his mahjong addiction more. Besides, when he was a general in Vietnam, he used his power to help my friend's business. He provided his jeep and soldiers to serve her family with things like picking up her kids from school and running errands for her mom. He also often collected debts for her from her debtors. His modest salary was also spent on the group's frivolous hobbies of weekend clubbing, so he had to take some more decoration soldiers' salaries. (Avoiding going to fight, some soldiers gave their salaries to the general and stayed home)

"Wait," I interrupted. "What group?"

"Her, her husband, her business friends, and I." Then as if he just remembered something, he lowered his voice.

"The time she asked me to collect money from you, I was truly reluctant. It was nothing compared to her high spending way of life. But I had to do what she asked. I just don't get her at all."

"It was nothing," I told him softly. "She helped me when I was in need. That's good enough. I am forever in debt to her."

Continuing his tearful story, he told me that the day he left in 1975, he brought my friend, her family, and even her friends with him. In America, he worked two jobs to take care of her. One time he was robbed while he was a clerk at a grocery store. They tied him up and pushed him to the ground. Since they were armed, he did not dare to resist, but felt shame nonetheless. He endured his difficulties for my friend because he loved her. But now she did not seem to feel the same. She gave him a week to move out. He accepted her falling out of love, as feelings cannot be forced. But what broke his heart was the fact that she told him she loved someone else.

Shocked, I went silent for a while.

"What are you going to do now?"

I have no idea. I'm hurt. I'm lost. I'm losing my mind," he replied. "I hate those who look down on my suffering. I'll follow Hoang Co Minh (a leader of the anti-Communist resistance) and take back the country. If I can regain my former position, she won't leave me. Please put in a word for me. I can't live without her."

It was my turn to be confused. I had to pick my words carefully to save him and others from future trouble.

I excused myself to get some tea, to think, and to then continue the story.

Coming back to the table, I looked him straight in the eye.

"I don't really like butting into others' business," I said calmly, but with a sense of finality.

"But if you came to me for an answer to your predicament, I will be frank with my opinion. I might offend you with my plain talk, but only an objective judgment can help you find your true calling. Will you listen to what I have to say?"

"I'm all ears," he said.

I began in a solemn voice.

"Honestly if I could, I would have told her not to associate with you before. But setting that morality aside, you should take hold of your chance to fix things now that you are given one. It's a natural part of being a human to make mistakes. The important thing is to realize your wrongdoing before judging someone else. Once you've realized the errors of your ways, fix them. I'm only talking about your life now because you came here to find me. I will not say a word to my friend."

"I understand," he said.

"According to my friend, your refugee ship leaving Vietnam in 1975 transported high-level officers and their families. I don't need to know exactly who. I just want you to tell me something. Is it true that when you reached the Philippines, you had to take off your uniforms and lower the yellow flag of the Republic, which was the only way the ship could refill fuel?

"That is true. It was painfully shameful wearing only my undershirt. I had no outer clothes with me except my uniform that I left aside."

I asked,

"Since the Philippine Army fought on our side, why did they insult you like that?"

He answered,

"Because we lost. I blame the Americans. We only asked for a couple hundred million more dollars, but they refused. That's why we lost."

"In my opinion, the reason why the Filipinos treated you like that was because at that moment, the Republic of Vietnam government and the yellow flag were things of the past. You yourself agreed when you took off your uniform and lowered the flag asking for help. Do you really believe that the Republic of Vietnam could have won with additional money? Have you ever wondered why the U.S. spent so much money and lost lives in battle, but refused a request for more money? I believe you know why."

The general remained silent. My question was unanswered.

"The U.S. had given so much money to South Vietnam, like weapons, uniforms, groceries, salaries, and even a pay raise when a child was born. Even if you did not have another child, you still got a pay raise if you submitted a false birth certificate to receive an additional grant to help you raise your nonexistent child. If you could not win the war with such help from the U.S,. how could you even imagine forming another army, let alone restore the country?"

Finally, he answered my question. "The Communist soldiers from the North fought wearing only an Ao Ba Ba and shorts, and just eating a handful of rice, and they won. We could do the same if we go back."

"They won because they had ideals and fought for justice. What did you have to motivate your men?" I asked.

The general gave me an angry answer. "The resentment of losing our country."

I disagreed. "You mean losing your important status and the power to rule. Vietnam was not lost as you say it was. It was liberated. It is now one country from North to South and is recognized by the world."

The atmosphere between us grew heavy. When I saw the general's mood, I was heartbroken. I lowered my voice sympathetically, but at the same time wanted to give him a wake-up call.

"I know you fell for my friend's beauty. Today you speak of shame, but really you have lived in shame for too long. As a general, you lost the pride of your uniform when you ran errands for her. When you departed the country, you took off your uniform and traded the yellow flag for help. Wasn't that shameful? Now that you're heartbroken and you think of winning back our country, you will be lying to yourself and to others just for a hopeless dream. You regret the things that you provided for her, but nothing can buy the honor of a man. That is something of value beyond money. What do you think about what I said?"

With his eyes closed and his hands clasped together

tightly as if giving himself strength, the general spoke slowly.

"You are right. I have nothing more to say, but I am in so much pain."

My words had influenced his thinking to some degree. I continued.

"Time heals all wounds, be it the body or the soul. You can stay here for the time being until you find a place to live. You can share meals with us. The kids go to school, and I work all day. You can rest and think carefully, calm down, then find a reasonable woman and establish a real family. It won't be difficult. For years you have traded your honor for a woman. Do you want to be dishonorable for the rest of your life? If my friend doesn't love you anymore, you should love yourself!"

Suddenly, he took my hand.

"Thank you," he choked. "Thank you very much. I will never forget your advice."

He stayed at our house for about a week before he found a new place to stay. He did not contact me again after that week. After a while, I heard his friends say that he sponsored a woman from the refugee camp. They got married and lived together until he died. The woman was lucky because she had the same name as my friend. I did not tell my friend about him visiting me. Only after his death I did tell her about it. She did not believe me at first, but when I told her the things that only the two of them knew, she knew that I was telling the truth.

Resettlement:
California — Vietnamese Community Issues

Unable to adjust to the weather in Maryland, three years later we moved to California. There was a large community of Vietnamese refugees in this state. I got along by helping new arrival Vietnamese with language difficulties. My apartment was next door to Aunt Bay's family. She lived with her younger brother and his two kids. They also escaped by boat like we did but they did not have any education, so I often helped when they were in need. Once we got to know each other more, she confided in me that she had a daughter who lived abroad that she could not see. The story was quite pitiful.

She said before 1975, her family lived in a small province. The governor there used his power to abuse her daughter. This happened to others also, but her daughter was luckier, maybe.

Because she was a skilled nurse, she was taken home by a big shot to serve in his house. The governor was unaffected even though the big shot had the power to take away his position or even imprison him. A short while before April 1975, the big shot's daughter was about to give birth in a foreign country. Auntie Bay's daughter was sent there to take care of the big shot's daughter. She did not return home. Auntie Bay had not heard from her daughter for a long time. The big shot wanted to stay out of sight in that country, so her daughter was not allowed to contact her own family.

Then one day the big shot's family moved to the US. He went on Vietnamese television here to criticize the US for abandoning the South, leading to his loss. Other big men used the same argument. No one dared to admit the truth. Since then, her daughter was allowed to contact the family by phone until Auntie fell ill. With her younger brother at work and no other relatives, I took care of her in the hospital as the family representative.

Test results showed that she had a severe stroke and would not survive. When I informed the daughter, she asked me to find a tailor to make a burial cloth according to the Cao Dai rite. But when the daughter finally arrived here, it was too late to see her mom before she passed away. While helping her dress up Auntie Bay's body, I looked closely at the face of the girl who had just lost her mother. Her gentle and naive nature was clear in her expression. "Thanks to my master and mistress," she whispered to me, "I was able to go home and attend my mother's funeral. How can I ever repay this debt to them?"

Suddenly, anger overwhelmed me. This girl's entire life had been taken over by powerful people. She was not allowed to have a home of her own. She could not take care of her mother in her sickness. They had deprived her of her own family relationships, and yet she still could not understand. I wanted to scream and tell her, but I held back because it was all too late.

There are many of our compatriots who are very loyal

to an individual with power. The nurse was an example. They feel proud to serve an authority figure, blind to the fact that they have been exploited to the core. Auntie Bay's brother worked for minimum wage in a noodle shop as a part of a franchise. He worked fourteen to fifteen hours a day, standing in water all day to the point of rotting his toenails. But he still happily did the drudgery work to help his boss save up to feed an imaginary army to win back the country. I asked him if he knew about the counter-revolution. He said he did not, but the boss did. How pitiful!

The nationalist or anti-Communist movements emerged in many forms just to collect money. Once I met a young acquaintance and heard that his father was highly active in fundraising programs. I asked him if he would participate.

He smiled and replied, "I don't know what kind of country restoration they think they are doing, which involves only a few gatherings, then drinking, dancing, and showing off fancy clothes. I had to be there to please my father. I don't want to make him mad but honestly, he's acting like a clown. I tell you this in confidence, so don't let him know, or otherwise I'll get disowned."

I sympathized with the young man because that is the truth about radical anti-Communist groups.

After a short while in California, I realized that the U.S. policy on social welfare was very lax. Most of the immigrants, including Vietnamese, took advantage of the loopholes to start a new life, from intellectuals to the working class. Vietnamese people as a class are smart, but at the same time, many will use their intelligence as a shortcut to illegal wealth. They outsmarted the system, but they lost the pride of Vietnamese culture. In times of difficulty, I had always been proud of my Vietnamese roots and lived according to those standards. I want to be respected for my way of life, not for the material things that I owned.

Living in a foreign land, I wished to be part of its society. Shortly after moving to California, I enrolled in a community college. It was extremely difficult since I had not been in school for so long. The English I had learned in high school was mostly forgotten, but I pushed myself to study till the end. I finally graduated with a degree in accounting and IT. The main motivation that helped me overcome all difficulties was self-esteem, since I did not have skillful hands nor the strength for other high-paying, labor-intensive jobs. I had only one plan: to get a degree to support my family. I was determined not to leech off American society.

I wanted to be close to my people to find spiritual connection. However, I was afraid to approach most of the Vietnamese people in the community. I did not join any church or organization. The reason was that I could not accept their attitudes about the current Vietnamese government. They had forgotten, or did not want to remember, that they once lived under a corrupt government. I did not like their dishonest way of life, so I lived a lonely life without friends because of my own point of view. When U.S./Vietnam relations were established, I was thrilled, longing for the day to return.

Return

In 1996, I returned for the first time with all the excitement and anxiety rolled into one. In the past, I had lost sleep many nights before I left Vietnam, as I did again, now. I had no idea how the government would treat a person who escaped out of the country. When I got off the plane, I was shivering with sweat, partly because of the hot climate, but mostly because of my emotions. Walking to the customs counter, I showed my passport and waited. The customs officer studied my passport closely and flipped the pages back and forth. My heart was pounding. Suddenly, he said something that I could not understand. First, it was because he spoke too fast. Second, the Northern accent was too strong. I am very familiar with the Northern accent but honestly, I didn't understand what he was saying. I asked him to repeat and to speak a little slower. Suddenly he shouted.

"How long have you been gone? Forgot even your own language?"

I trembled even more, unsure what to do. The guilt of having left my country before had shocked me. Some Vietnamese who had arrived before me saw what happened to me and gave me a sign that the officer was looking for tips, so I immediately pushed a five-dollar-bill next to my passport. He grabbed it quickly, stamped my passport, and gave it back to me with a smile. After completing the immigration procedure, I staggered out of the airport terminal.

In the following days, I paid visits to relatives near and far. I will never forget when I visited my uncle to ask forgiveness for leaving the country. He was not angry and showed sympathy. He stroked my head, eyes gazing into the distance. Out of nowhere, he told me to remember my grandparents' names, my father's name, and his name. I realized that he was old and his mind was declining. I hugged him tight, as if trying to hold on to something from the past.

I visited Aunt Hai's family, tearfully. She had grown old. When I asked, she told me that Be, her daughter, died when run over by a garbage truck as she was collecting plastic bags at a dumpster. Auntie and her two sons put up a house near the canal, better than the old hut, but they were still dirt poor. The weather was very hot.

Auntie asked me,

"Do you want to lie down with me? There is no hammock for you, but you can rest here. It's so hot."

I smiled wordlessly and picked up the pillow on a worn-out mat to lie down next to Auntie on the old bed. Auntie waved a paper fan to cool me, and we continued telling the difficult stories of our lives like the old days. I asked about the lieutenant colonel's family and learned that Ms. Kham had died of an illness during the difficult years of the country. The lieutenant colonel had gone to the U.S. (all officers from the Republic, after they were released from re-education camp, immigrated to America under the Humanitarian Operation). Their daughter was now married to a rich officer who was working at the customs seaport, living in a lavish house several times bigger than her parents' house.

"Hey, I have seen people who immigrated to the U.S. and they got rich fast, so why do you still look like us commoners?" Auntie suddenly asked me.

"What about you?" I laughed, and asked her, "I heard that revolutionist families now are loaded, so why are you still living like this?" Auntie smiled a gentle, toothless smile.

"Oh well! It's probably because we don't know how to get rich."

After a week, I left Vietnam feeling bittersweet. During my stay, I was swindled everywhere I went: the taxi driver, the market, and the food vendors. They treated me like a foreigner. It seemed like all they cared about was my money, even though I had returned because of love. I also learned that many overseas Vietnamese who returned before I did had not been honest. They gave the people in Vietnam an illusion that making money in the U.S. was easy. So when I confessed that my civil servant salary was only enough to scrape by, everyone thought I was lying.

Admiration of foreigners was still heavy in the field of customer service. A typical example would be on a flight from Taiwan to Vietnam. When the plane had just taken off, a Vietnamese flight attendant held a stack of foreign newspapers to hand out to interested passengers. When she walked by me, I saw some English newspapers and raised my hand to signal that I wanted one. The flight attendant ignored me as she continued to offer newspapers to Westerners. When she came by again, I signaled again to her. She walked past me without stopping.

Angry, I shouted,

"Excuse me!" She turned to look at me with a cold expression.

"What do you want?" she asked.

"I want to read the newspaper. Why didn't you give me one? I raised my hand twice, but you still pretended to see nothing."

"We do not have a newspaper written in Vietnamese," she told me.

"Do you assume that I don't know English? And even if I don't know English, I can still look at the pictures. All passengers should be treated with courtesy, so why are you welcoming to Western passengers and being rude to me? This attitude of pampering foreigners and looking down on our people I have seen too much of under the old regime. You live under the new era but still act like before. The state must educate you better. Now bring the newspaper. We can read it together to see if you understand better than I do. If you don't give me a paper, I will report this to the chief of staff of the airline."

Just then, another flight attendant, probably the supervisor, heard the incident and came to apologize. The face of the girl passing out newspapers went pale, and she started stammering, something I could not make out. For the rest of the flight, flight attendants took turns asking if I needed anything. I am, in fact, a very easy-going passenger. I just wanted equality in treatment. That attendant judged me by the plain clothes I was wearing, something that should not be done in modern society.

Scent of the Sea

Back in the U.S., although busy with life, my mind was heavy with worries. I thought about the negativities in my native land with sympathy. I did not criticize, as I had no right. I thought of myself as a daughter in a family who went to work far away, and upon returning realized her parents had grown tired and that her siblings had lost their way on their life paths. I wondered what I should do to help my family over there.

As trading between Vietnam and the U.S. became easier, there was more negativity. The frauds for love and money between the Vietnamese who lived overseas and the Vietnamese in Vietnam scared me. Now the advice of my father and my teachers to love our people made me confused.

In 2005, I retired from my position in the accounting department of the school district, leaving me with plenty of free time, so I decided to travel around Asia, including Vietnam, on a Princess Cruise. I still remember clearly that moonless night when the vast sky and sea were pitch dark. I was sitting in a deck chair when I smelled the familiar scent drifting over the sea. I ran up to the pilot house to ask the captain,

"Has the ship arrived in Vietnam already?"

"How did you know?" the captain asked in surprise.

"Yes, we have just entered the waters of Vietnam. How could you tell?"

"I can't see land," I answered in a voice that sounded more like a cheer, "but I can smell my homeland."

All at once, a warm feeling filled my soul, the feeling of my childhood days when my parents and grandmother held me in their arms. Tears came and I cried like a baby. So, this is patriotism. Father, I understand now.

Grains of Sand

Returning to the U.S., I kept wondering. I always bought a lot of gifts for my loved ones in Vietnam when I visited them, but that was not the point. The important thing was how I could help improve their lives, which was such a tremendous objective that I did not know where to start.

At the beginning of 2006, I was diagnosed with breast cancer. Honestly, I was not scared upon hearing the news. I had a strong faith in the fate of people, so on the contrary, I was very calm. I spent a lot of time reflecting on the duties and responsibilities of a human being, and I realized that I had done everything in my power for my family. My children had grown up, and both sides of my relatives were well taken care of. The only important thing left was that I had not done anything for my homeland. I spent many sleepless nights thinking about this; I found it overwhelming with limited powers.

Then I thought of my father, and of the song "Where Have Our Old friends Gone?" and of his dying words for me, of his thin figure on the bicycle with his breadbasket, the packages he exchanged with strangers, his bloody face upon coming home, and the soldier dragging him out of bed and throwing him on the ground. What he did was not so much. He did not have a rank. He died quietly. In the struggle for independence when so many had sacrificed, father was just one more grain of sand. But he contributed that grain of sand to build a foundation for a successful fight.

I am the daughter of a grain of sand. I too am a grain of sand. I will dedicate this grain to benefit my homeland. Enough waiting, I will share the rest of my life with my people. If I can help to make a few changes in their lives, I will be satisfied. I feel like a person in a dark tunnel suddenly seeing a way out.

Helping Hand

In May 2006, I had surgery, and ended radiation therapy in August 2006. In September 2006, I returned to Vietnam. I had a relative who lived in Hamlet 5, Xuan Thoi Son Commune, Hoc Mon District. I chose this place as a landmark. I went to see the noticeably young hamlet chief, and asked him about the situation of the people there. He told me the difficulties they faced: how he was concerned about children dropping out of school too early, and that most of their parents were in the working class. The neighborhood had not yet developed, so access was difficult. He said the hamlet included ten groups of households. From each group, I asked the group leaders to help me choose two children from underprivileged families who were eager to study. I would give them a one-year scholarship so that they did not have to drop out of school.

So in 2007, I started out giving scholarships to twenty children in the hamlet. At first, I thought that I should try to help the children finish high school. Thinking that they also needed some English in case they wanted to find work in restaurants or hotels in the city, as the number of foreign tourists coming to our country was on the rise, I started a class and hired an English teacher. When the students were about to graduate, I started a class to tutor math for them. What excited me was that they continued to university; some for two years, some for four years, depending on their ability.

During this time, I always stood by them in all the ways I could. In addition to returning every year to grant scholarships, I used email and phone calls to regularly counsel them from far away and to encourage them when they were in need. When they were sick, I took care of hospital fees and medicine. I provided food monthly to those children without parents. One year, dengue fever plagued the city and many people ended up in the hospital. I hired cleaners to clean up the canals in the neighborhood and spray insecticides to help relieve the people's suffering. I was in a momentum that I could not stop.

In addition to the children, I also took care of adults, buying land to build houses for people in need, and offering full scholarships in vocational schools for older children to learn a trade to help support their families. Every Tet Holiday, I prepared gifts for underprivileged families, and basic food for them to enjoy on the three days of the Lunar New Year.

At first, people in the hamlet thought I was doing some kind of business to earn favors from the government. But once they saw that I did not invest in anything, but just kept pouring money into helping people, then the government suspected that I had a political scheme. I asked for a meeting with the authorities to explain myself: I simply felt for my compatriots. That was all. At a meeting with the people, someone asked me if I did this for good karma so I could go to heaven or nirvana after death. I replied that I had yet to meet anyone returning from the dead, so I had no idea about those places. The only thing I asked was that people did not call me a Viet Kieu (a Vietnamese person who lives in a foreign country). That term made me feel distant. I had felt enough loneliness in America, so here in my country, I just wanted to be among my people, and have them please just call me by my name.

Every year when I go to the hamlet to grant scholarships, in my speeches I always call for solidarity, love, and kindness. Sometimes my tearful words make many officials emotional. I use myself as an example so the youth can follow. I remind them that the value of the word "freedom" goes hand in hand with "responsibility." They must understand this properly. Once in a meeting with the children, a question was raised about the law and the rights of the people in the U.S. I answered honestly, which surprised them.

"In my opinion, people here in Vietnam have more freedom than in America."

They looked at each other, and one of them asked,

"What do you mean by that? I don't understand."

"Let me give you a simple example," I replied. "Here, people are free to throw garbage and free to defecate wherever it suits them. And people are free to drive any way they want, regardless of the law. In the U.S, there is no such freedom. And if anyone violates the law, the penalty is very heavy. I tell you this so that you can understand the true meaning of the word freedom. You ask about freedom, but no one has asked me about the responsibility of the people. You should learn good things from the West to improve society here, and at the same time preserve our beautiful customs and traditions. Do not criticize the government, but ask yourself whether you have complied with your responsibilities as a citizen or not."

Understanding

During my comings and goings to the hamlet, I researched about Ho Chi Minh's life. I remember one time Mr. Sau, the hamlet secretary, showed me a book about Uncle Ho's teachings for the morality of party members. I was touched. I asked him for the book but he refused, saying he could not let that book out of his hands. Returning to the U.S., I went to the library to learn more about Uncle Ho. The more I read, the more respect and pride I had for Ho Chi Minh.

The more I learned about the Vietnam War, the more I loved my people. One thing I noted, however, was that no one mentioned the past in Vietnam. In my opinion, the history of the struggle leading to unification and peace must be remembered. The next generations must know the sacrifices of those who have gone before, must know the value of independence and freedom, and what it will take to protect their country from foreign interference.

I heard about 18 Vuon Trau Village, a citadel against our enemies. I think that place wasn't too far from Giong T-Junction. I put a bookcase in the hamlet headquarters and put many books in it about that neighborhood and the history of their struggle. I wanted my students to read these books. Then I held a contest with prizes to see what my students had learned.

Once the embargo was lifted, I understood that it was natural how people needed to find all kinds of ways to make life more prosperous after a long time living in poverty. It was not wrong to look at the more developed countries and follow their success so that we too kept up with other world civilizations. But I also wanted to hold onto what I considered to be the historic characteristics of the Vietnamese, because that was the rich value of our nation.

As the number of students in need increased, my finances dwindled. When I first came back, I stayed at the Grand Hotel on Dong Khoi Street, a four-star hotel. Eventually I had to move, so I went to the Thien Xuan Hotel, a two-star hotel on Le Thanh Ton Street where I returned to ever since. The security guards knew me well. Once they asked me why every time I returned, I only went to Hoc Mon and Phu Nhuan, while our country had many other beautiful destinations. I laughed and did not answer.

The truth was that I went to Phu Nhuan to visit my uncle. Although he no longer knew what was going on around him, he always remembered my grandparents' names, my father's name, and his own name. A very strange thing was every time I came back, I bought him some food and fed him myself. He ate everything happily. When I left, he held my hand, reluctant to let go. The last time I could take care of him was in 2011, with the promise that I would return next year. My uncle passed away in August 2012.

Speaking of traveling within the country, if I wanted

to visited the sights, I would run out of money to help people in Hoc Mon. But the future of the children was more important. That is a choice that made the rest of my days more meaningful. As time passed, in the following ten years, there were occasionally things that required my returning to Vietnam. But I never stayed long. I noticed that although the country had many positive changes, many negativities persisted.

I have had a dispute since 2007 with the people who illegally took over my late mother's house after she and my grandmother passed. The Court of First Instance and Court of Appeal in Ho Chi Minh City ruled that I lost, even though I had documents and lawyers to back up my family claim. During the trial, my lawyer stood silently to hear the verdict with no argument. But I did not give up. I appealed to the Supreme People's Court in Hanoi. I was beyond surprised and touched when I received the decision from the Supreme People's Court that overturned my loss in the lower courts.

Patriots?

One day by chance in America, I met a girl from my high school in Vietnam who was a few years younger than me. When she found out what I was doing in Vietnam, she introduced me to a group of "patriots." I had lived away from the Vietnamese community for so long that I did not know of any organizations. Now that I knew there were people like me who cared for the country, I was glad. I went to their meetings to learn about how they helped our people.

This organization consisted of intellectuals who organized presentations, and each session connected with other places in the world where Vietnamese have settled. Each "patriot" announced his former position in the Republic regime. They belonged to a branch of another famous organization that I had often heard about. I wondered why they opted for a new name instead of the original name. After a few meetings, I understood their purpose but still listened patiently. They used the idea of patriotism to raise money from people like me, then took that money supposedly to distribute to underprivileged young people in Vietnam. They painted a picture of heaven in America. They encouraged the young people to stand up against the current government, and if they were imprisoned, the organization would help get them released to go to America.

At the third meeting, the chairperson wanted to hear my opinion because I had sat quietly in all the meetings. I told them if they really wanted to hear my opinion, would they please let me speak at the next meeting, and I would prepare more carefully. I came back the next week. Everyone was very eager to hear what I had to say.

"First of all," I started gently, "I apologize in advance because I know my words might upset the people here, but at the same time, I look forward to hearing criticism to better myself." The room suddenly fell silent. Everyone looked at me, waiting to hear my next words.

"Ladies and gentlemen," I continued, "the things I say here will undoubtedly be controversial, but there is only one thing that we and the entire world agree on that is, in other words, unchangeable, and that is the definition of the word Vietnam.

"So, what is Vietnam? Well, it is a country with territory, sovereignty, history, customs, language, and more than four thousand years of civilization. The government body is the Socialist Republic under the leadership of the Communist Party. With such understanding, what is Vietnam to us here in America? A foreign country? A place where we travel? A place where we do business? Or is it still our homeland?

"If it is our homeland, then is Vietnam the past, the present, or the future to us? If it is our past, then who are we now? American, French, Australian? If it is our present, what do we know about the life, thoughts, and dreams of our compatriots in Vietnam? If it is our future, what will we and must we contribute to the development of the country?

"For me, Vietnam is my past, my present, and my future. That's why I would like to express my thoughts and hopes to you all. If we have the same patriotism and solidarity between us and our compatriots, that is what our country needs. It cannot be built on antagonism and hatred.

"1. The first thing I want is the yellow flag (the Republic flag) to rest in peace to preserve its remaining bit of honor. You shall not use that flag for your own purposes. Today, the red flag representing our country in the world must be respected.

"2. I don't call April 30, 1975, the "Day of Hate," as you call it. I call it Liberation and Reunification Day.

"3. Do not say we have lost our country because our country is still there, one whole stretch from North to South. Institutions might have changed in Vietnam, but we Vietnamese are still the same.

"4. The house we were living in collapsed for reasons we do not need to know. And we want to rebuild it the same as it was before, using old tools, old materials, and old expert builders. That is absurd. If people were indeed happy under the Republican regime, why would they demand change? The Southern Liberation Front is a good example of the desire for change.

"5. If we talk about hatred, we must direct it to France, Japan, and even Thailand. Countless Vietnamese have died at their hands, but we are willing to forget the past. We praise and use their goods. We travel and spend money in those countries. On the contrary, we hate our people of the same race, to the point that we never want to set foot back on our ancestral homeland. We would rather buy Chinese products than Vietnamese. You say, 'Let them die.' Who are *they*? Aren't they our blood brothers?

"6. We live in comfort here but go out of our way to encourage our brothers in Vietnam, who are still foolish and willing to go to jail just for a few dollars. We want to see blood spilled, but whose blood? After so many years of bloodshed into streams, just now can our siblings enjoy peace. Why do we want to cause chaos? For my last words, I want to say that if we no longer have even a shred of love for our homeland, we can still enjoy our new life. That is well within our rights. But we have no right to interfere and destroy the peaceful life of our brothers and sisters back at home."

There was not a single objection to my words. I was not sure why. Maybe they thought I was too low to argue with, because who was I but a mere commoner? But at the end of the meeting, when I was walking to my car, the chairperson came over and invited me to his house for further explanation of the group's activities. He first asked about my activities in Vietnam, to which I said that I was currently providing scholarships to students and helping their families in tough times. But most importantly, I was inspiring patriotism and solidarity in them.

He wanted to know how I could do such things, and what the relationship was between me and the local government. I let him know that the first stage was not easy because I was not doing business, but simply sponsoring students. That raised many questions with the authorities about my purpose, but like everything in this world, time would prove my innocent purpose.

Although he had heard my thoughts on Vietnam, he still tried to convince me to work with his group. He told me that he was able to connect with many young people in the country who painted on the walls of public places and distributed T-shirts with the words H.S., (Hoang Sa), T.S. (Truong Sa), and V.N. (Vietnam). These were known as the Paracel and Spratly Islands. I asked for the purpose of such actions, to which he explained that the two islands of Hoang Sa and Truong Sa had belonged to Vietnam, but the state sold them to China. The whole country would also be handed over to China in 2020 so now they must encourage the people to reclaim the islands and keep the Chinese government off our borders. To do that, it would take money to send people back to Vietnam. He hoped I would contribute to a cause greater than what I was doing. I looked at him and thought, "This man underestimates me!"

Seeing my lack of response, he added,

"I know you are patriotic, but if you only take care of the poor, you will get nowhere. You can't do anything alone, either. I advise you to cooperate with us. As you have seen, this is a collaboration of Vietnamese people around the world. We must act quickly; otherwise we will be unable to keep up. Once the Chinses Communist Party seizes control, it will be difficult to get the country back."

I did not argue with him because I realized his purpose in inviting me to his house. Before leaving, I told him that I would email him my decision. When he saw me off, he rushed across the garden to pick a grapefruit and handed it to me, smiling and patting me on the shoulder.

"For you, the first fruit of the season, very precious," he said.

"Thank you. Sorry, I have nothing to give you," I replied

"It's no big deal. See you at the meeting next week. Goodbye!"

The next day, I sent him an email. I said that I did not want to sabotage his or the group's work, and in my opinion, all of us Vietnamese love Vietnam, especially those living abroad. But each express that love according to their own feelings and experiences. He and I will go on two different paths, but if we both look to our country with unconditional love, one day all of us, the Viet children, will meet in the motherland of Vietnam.

Compatriotism

On my trips between the U.S. and Vietnam, I always wished for a friend to accompany me, so I always told my acquaintances in the U.S. about the changes in Vietnam. They did not react but gradually shunned me, saying I left for Vietnam as a "Viet Kieu" (a Viet living overseas), but now returned as a "Viet Cong" (member of the National Liberation Front of South Vietnam) because I was brainwashed. When I praised the steady course on which the Communist Party and the state had steered Vietnam, they thought I was "brownnosing" the Communists. I replied that it would be an honor for me to take care of the leaders when they become too old and weak, to repay the favor. What could be more precious? They thought I had gone crazy, so the friendships always ended there.

Living separate from the Vietnamese community, my only comfort was the success of the students in Vietnam. To this day, I do not remember how many students received my support in almost every profession, including doctors, engineers, nurses, teachers, accountants, tailors, cosmetologists, etc. Some are married with children. Notably, there were two who met in my sponsorship program, fell in love, and are now married with two kids.

In 2015, my sponsorship program was still going, but I had to face the fact that my finances were running out. I was frustrated because making money at my age was practically a pipedream. This meant that soon I would have to stop the work I was doing in Vietnam. I informed the students and teachers to prepare them mentally. Then, in my search for a companion, I met an American. Amid our stories about the meaning of life through which I honestly confessed my feelings, what surprised me was that he was very understanding and sympathetic with my patriotism. He realized that I loved Vietnam very much, but I had not had the opportunity to see the reality of the country. He was willing to sponsor a trip from North to South for me as a birthday present.

So I returned to Vietnam to rent a car. Traveling with me was the driver and the car owner. We set out from Ho Chi Minh City along the national highways heading to the North. In addition to the natural scenery, which made everyone who passed through be in awe of its beauty, I personally experienced the love for my fellow human beings, which touched me deep within my soul and made me love our people more.

When I went to Ly Son Island, I met a taxi driver from the North. I found it strange because the rest of the island was just locals. Turned out he was transferred to be stationed in Ly Son back when he was in the army and he fell in love with the island and a girl living there. So when he was discharged from the army, he chose to stay and settle down there. Knowing that we were going to visit Lao Cai, he quickly introduced us to his cousin and her husband from Lao Cai to show us around. When we arrived, the young couple was already welcoming and took us to a specialty restaurant in a leaf hut with a big fishpond. I fished for myself, and the owner made the dish for me. While eating, I mentioned a song that I really liked but the name escaped me. I was humming a few lines when the wife cheered.

"Oh, I know! It's called "Sea, Nostalgia and You."

While eating, the couple asked to learn more about me. I told them I was seventy and showed them a copy of my passport, accidentally letting them know that it was my birthday that day. The couple pulled each other over to the corner of the garden for a while. When they came back, they told me to go with them to this cool place after dinner. When we got there, the surprise they gave me made me cry: a birthday cake with my name on it, and my favorite song being played in a cozy room at the restaurant.

The next day we went to visit Ham Rong Mountain, Sapa, at an altitude of eighteen hundred meters. The two told me that the mountain was too high and I should just look it, but not bother climbing it as it would be too exhausting. But I was determined to climb, so the couple decided they would follow in case I got tired, so there would be someone there to carry me down. We reached the top and came back safely, and the two of them sighed out of relief because they were so worried. What really touched my heart was when I asked about their compensation, they refused to accept my money.

"We are not rich, but we can treat you to meals and experiences like this," one of them said to me. "We are merchants and we love money, but sometimes compatriot love is far more precious."

We parted with much reluctance, and when I returned to the U.S., I bought a fishing rod to send back as a gift to the couple to commemorate a meaningful meeting, and hoped one day I could return to Lao Cai to visit my two precious friends again.

In April 2016, I received a phone call from Aunt Hai's family from Vietnam. She wanted to talk to me. My instinct told me something bad had happened. "Aunt Hai?" I answered quickly.

"I'm here, how are you?" A faint voice on the other end of the line made my heart ache.

"I probably won't make it, Miss. You stay strong, my most cherished friend. I want to say goodbye to you before I go."

I choked. "Auntie Hai, I love you very much. Thank you for being a part of my life. If there is a next life, I hope I will see you again."

She replied, "That would be great. But will our next life be better or just as bad as this life, Miss?"

"Good or bad makes no difference, as long as we meet again, Aunt Hai. Don't forget me," I said, laughing but with tears in my eyes.

"Don't you forget me either."

Stomach cancer had robbed Aunt Hai of her life, but my love for her will always live on. Her image will live on in my work for the less fortunate people in my home country. Auntie and I weren't just friends—we were comrades.

Back to Roots

All my children and grandchildren have visited Vietnam many times except for my youngest, who left the country at the age of three. My children grew up in an entirely American community. I separated us from the rest of the Vietnamese community lest they be affected by radical anti-Communist movements. And for that reason, I did not send them to Vietnamese language classes. However, my three older kids still speak, read, and write Vietnamese, but the three younger ones are more fluent in speaking only. When my youngest was forty years old, he quietly returned to Vietnam without telling me. He told his siblings to hide the fact from me because he wanted to learn about Vietnam without being influenced by others' ideals.

When he returned, we had a meal together. At that time, when I found out about what he did, I was pleasantly surprised. The whole family was eager to hear his story.

I quickly asked, "

How was it? How long was the trip? Where did you go? Were there any problems? How was the food?"

He laughed at my onslaught of questions and replied happily, "I spent two weeks and visited from North to South. I ate at street-side food stalls or at any crowded place, I went in."

"Why eat on the street? Were you conscious about not spending too much?"

"Not quite. I wanted to meet and interact with local people to learn more.

What I loved the most was eating with the older folks, common folks. They liked me a lot."

"What language did you speak?" I asked.

"Entirely Vietnamese, Mother. Southern, Central, Northern. I understood everything," he replied.

"What did you think about Vietnam?" I asked him. He pondered the question for a moment.

"You know," he answered, his voice full of emotion, "I have traveled the whole world, but I have never felt as special as when I was in Vietnam."

"How come, Son?"

"When I opened my eyes, I saw people like me. And when I closed my eyes, I could smell a remarkably familiar scent that only exists in Vietnam. I left the country when I was three years old, yet that scent lingers in my mind. How strange, I don't understand. What do you think?"

"I understand how you feel. I have also experienced it, the scent of our homeland."

Suddenly, his girlfriend lifted his sleeve for everyone to see. On his right arm was a tattoo of a detailed map of Vietnam.

The meal that day was bustling with discussions among my children about beautiful places they had visited in Vietnam, good places to eat, and an itinerary for the family to visit together was also planned.

Reality

Sometimes I wonder why there are some Vietnamese who have not returned to Vietnam since 1975. They did not live under the regime for a day, yet they hold such prejudices against the current Vietnamese government. In the past, people who left the country had their own reasons, mostly poverty, including my family. After 1995, the sanctions were abolished. The party and state changed their policies and guidelines to promote economic development, improve living standards, bring happiness and prosperity to people's lives, from urban to rural areas. I have gone back many times since 1996. I have witnessed, and the world has also recognized, the positive changes in the economy of Vietnam.

Life in mountainous and remote areas was still difficult, partly because of the influence of customs. Radical anti-Communists used these circumstances to find fault with the government, forgetting the fact that they were comparing a developed country to another still developing counterpart.

I thought of an air force officer in the former Republic of Vietnam. I heard that he was quite an educated man. Once he acted in a spectacular anti-Communist play that made him a hero among the anti-Communists in the U.S. But then for a while his performance became shameless, so his limelight was cut. He disappeared from the stage, scraping by somewhere, living on a homeless provision. Then one day, knowing his death was drawing near, he reappeared, making the same anti-Communist argument. He used his last bit of wisdom to find himself a grave, because he had no place to call home. He was finally satisfied when a radical anti-Communist group that was looking for a hero, jumped at the opportunity to organize a funeral for him. I heard it was quite grand and elaborate, and was enough for them to show off to the world that they just buried their hero.

I am not opposed to his previous actions as they had nothing to do with me. But when he attacked a singer of his children's age from Vietnam performing in the U.S., I saw it as immoral. Just as when he claimed to be the representative of all overseas Vietnamese, I could not accept the claim because he did not represent me.

To repay America, twice a week I volunteered to cook for about two hundred homeless Americans who lived huddled under filthy bridges with rats. Once a year, we would knit hats and socks, or ask for old clothes and shoes from other people to donate to the homeless. Winter times were miserable. Even with our provided blankets, they still had to sleep near the city sewer at times to keep warm. The number of homeless people kept rising, with more beggars on the streets. The sad thing was that in recent years, I had seen us Vietnamese among the beggars. I wondered how they were able to settle down in the U.S., who got them here, and for what reason they ended up broke on the street?

After more than forty years since unification, Vietnam's historic progress has been recognized by the world. Some Vietnamese living abroad still hate the state and refuse to return, as they no longer enjoy the same privileges they used to get from the American aid before. Or perhaps reality was too contrary to the propaganda spewed among their community, so they didn't have the honest understanding to face the truth.

Why did I ask my people to let the old yellow flag rest in peace? Today, in the eyes of some Americans, the yellow flag only reminds them of a dark period in history that they want to forget. American soldiers returning home from Vietnam were rejected by their own people, many unable to stand the humiliation, and ending up mentally disabled. They could not return to their normal lives. What horrified them the most was when they saw the yellow flag and the American flag together. Under both flags there were Vietnamese people in military uniforms. There was no honor. Some even thought it was a form of protest, as the yellow flag followed the U.S. and lost, so it must be here to serve as a reminder. People only celebrate and commemorate glorious victories, but the anti-Communists here did the opposite. This was the story of some Americans I have encountered. When they knew that I, too, despised the yellow flag, they sincerely told me about their suffering.

Recently, the radical anti-Communist groups came up with a new method. In every American protest about partisan struggles, the yellow flag would be raised with the hope of being acknowledged. I was ashamed to see the flag holders get kicked out of the group because after all, that was the flag under which I grew up. On the contrary, there were Americans who, when running for election in a neighborhood with many Vietnamese, liked to use the flag to win votes. But when the job was done, the flag was unceremoniously cast away.

America's political climate is changing unpredictably. If we want to intervene to support or oppose a party, we should do it under the American flag. This is the United States of America, and we are American citizens. Please do not use the yellow flag. It no longer represents any country in the world. What worries me is that one day the flag will be listed as representing a group of extremists or terrorists. If that happens, it will be very heartbreaking. After all, I'm still Vietnamese. I hope we all expand our horizons before we act so we will not have any regrets.

Word to My Compatriots

My work over the past fifteen years has never been to publicize my name or to get famous. My dream is to dedicate the rest of my life to my homeland with all that I can. With the support of my husband, I will try to bring some small amount of happiness to my people, and at the same time find the meaning of my own life. That is why I choose to live in silence. Many times, the local government has offered to promote me to the district or the city by giving me a certificate of merit, which I have always refused. That was never my purpose. My intention is to create and multiply kindness. I am a commoner who has lived through many regimes, and I have never seen my country as peaceful as it is today. I would like to send a message to the Vietnamese who have been living overseas since the day they left our homeland. You should visit our country once to have a clearer view of yourself. And I urge my compatriots in Vietnam to stay vigilant against external propaganda about a heaven that never existed, even in a powerful country like the United States.

Some negativities may remain in Vietnam, but we will work together to tackle it with a sense of responsibility and learn from neighboring countries how to reform ours, but not to rely on foreign forces. No country loves another country more than it loves itself. When I talk with foreigners, they always praise us Vietnamese people for our incredible wit, diligence, and skills. We should utilize all those advantages to create uniquely Vietnamese cultural products.

Why do we have to imitate other people? They got ahead because they built their economy on their own national foundation. We also have our own national pride. More than that, we have an incredibly heroic history. If the Vietnamese in and out of the country joined hands, I believe our nation would one day be on par with the giants.

I have met many American tourists in Vietnam. When they knew that I was Vietnamese, they happily complimented our country about everything from the scenery to the people. Some even returned more than once with separate groups of friends. But personally, the traveling experience I had in Israel gave me unforgettable joy.

At the beginning of 2019, my husband and I were invited by a group of Jewish intellectuals to visit their homeland. Upon entering the hotel, when the secretary realized that I was Vietnamese, she embraced me, overjoyed. She told me that she had just returned from a one-month visit to Vietnam. I was curious as to why she stayed for a month. I asked her what in Vietnam had made her so excited. She said it was the beautiful scenery and delicious food, but especially the people. Wherever she went, she saw friendly smiles from people in a peaceful atmosphere. That was something she could not find in Israel. If she did not have to go back to work, she would have extended her stay to enjoy the happiness that we Vietnamese have fortunately found for ourselves.

In the following days when we toured the whole country, I understood why the secretary loved Vietnam so much. During the farewell party, some friends had questions for me. They wanted to know how Vietnam could bounce back so quickly after all the difficulties we all had suffered.

Proudly, I answered,

"Well, it is thanks to the wise leadership of the party and state, who understood the situation needed to change for the people's hearts. Moreover, while we have not forgotten the past, we also do not hold grudges. We are willing to make friends with former enemies and move forward together for a better future."

"Communism in Europe has collapsed. What ideology does Vietnam follow now to allow its rapid development?" an Israeli friend still wondered.

I smiled. "Honestly, I don't know anything about politics, so I can't really answer this question. But in my opinion, the party and state have applied the ideology of Ho Chi Minh, the godfather of our nation that we worship."

When we left Israel to return to America. I brought with me an indescribable joy about Vietnam.

These days, I feel happy and proud of my nation, but anxious at the same time. My biggest fear is that since the country is developing so fast, those who keep up will lead a prosperous life, while on the contrary, people who for distinct reasons fail to keep up will be left behind and classism will re-emerge in society. In my understanding, Ho Chi Minh's fight was not only for independence, but also for social equality. My second biggest fear is that the younger generation is indifferent to the history of the nation's struggle. If they do not learn the meaning of their predecessors' sacrifices, eventually we will lose that sense of vigilance and patriotism.

I believe that under the brilliant leadership of our party and state, new ideologies and policies will be put in place to move the country forward without losing our spiritual and cultural values. May everyone love and care for each other so that we can share the sweet fruit in the garden that Uncle Ho cultivated. I am but an expatriate child who loves the country in silence with the dream of a powerful Vietnam, which will stand side by side the most powerful countries across five continents in the near future.

My purpose for this disclosure, which I have kept hidden for many years, is that I want to call on my fellow Vietnamese Americans: please do not buy into the wonderful words of organizations hidden under the guise of patriotism, to raid and disturb the peaceful life of our compatriots living now in Vietnam. Those organizations paint a heavenly picture, but it is just a fantasy of how things were in the past. I want to call on all my brothers living abroad to cast away your personal hatred of forces that caused us to leave our land, as we share the same blood and history. And even if we do not give a hand rebuilding the country, please do not tear it down.

Epilogue: My Story

Time flies. Soon enough, my years living in America were longer than in Vietnam, but I never considered myself an American. I was always consciously thinking this was not my homeland. I was a mere guest. But with more than thirty-five years of citizenship, my children and I are good citizens of the U.S. My husband was a JAG officer in the American National Guard. He has fully supported me in helping my compatriots back home. I thank the Americans for giving my family the opportunity to have a stable life. And though this is the current state of my life, in my heart I can never truly be American. I have never been a part of America's history, but my country's history is soaked with American blood from a war which could have been avoided.

I am proud of the fighting spirit of my people. I also sympathize with the suffering that the families of fifty-eight-thousand American soldiers who died on that remote "pissant" land, must have gone through. The consequence of that war is that both sides lost, both the winner and the loser, both the powerful and the "pissant." And the pain did not stop when the war ended. It persists in the bodies and souls of those who participated in the war, sometimes across generations, such as the victims of Agent Orange. With my age and life experiences through different regimes, I believe that common people in this world always want peace. They all want to have a stable life so they can take care of their family, raise their children, watch them grow and become adults, and now rest and enjoy their grandchildren. It does not matter where you come from—a different ethnic group, another diverse culture, a small or large country. We all share the same dream.

I am ending my story with happy news. On Sep 10 and 11, 2023, President Biden visited Vietnam. He had meetings with General Secretary Nguyen Phu Trong, and President Vo Van Thuong. They signed an agreement to make the relationship between Vietnam and America a "Comprehensive Strategic Partnership."

President Biden brought back to America a special gift from President Vo Van Thuong—a book titled "One Person, One Path, and One History: Ho Chi Minh—Letters to America." All the letters were written by Ho Chi Minh to the American people, from the presidents down to young students. The letters were dated June 18, 1919, to August 25, 1969, seven days before he passed away. In those letters, Ho Chi Minh always showed our yearning for independence, peace, and friendship, and it finally came after a long painful history for both sides.

But we will embrace and celebrate the future in harmony together, starting today. I do hope this relationship will heal the wounds of the souls of the people who were sacrificed in the Vietnam War. Respect for the sovereignty of all is vital for world peace and common prosperity.

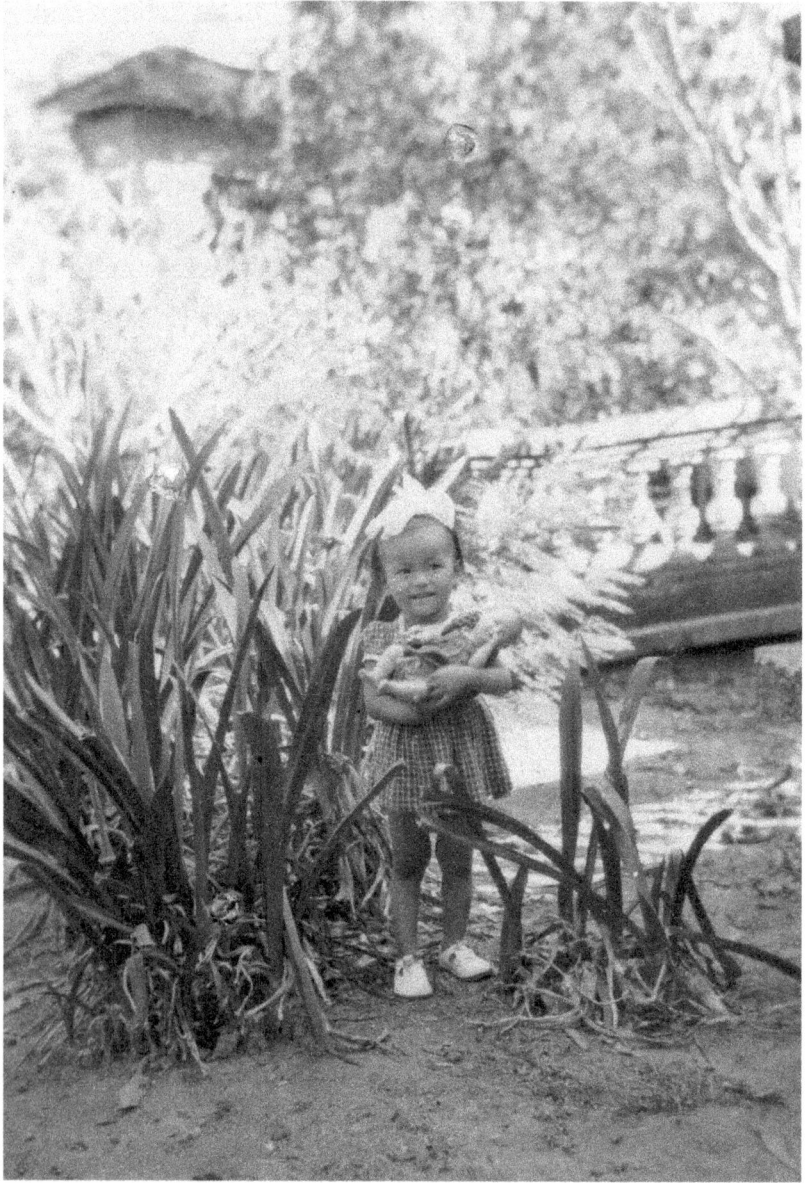

Mai McBride holding a doll with blue eyes

Youngest brother in front of the house in Ban Co City

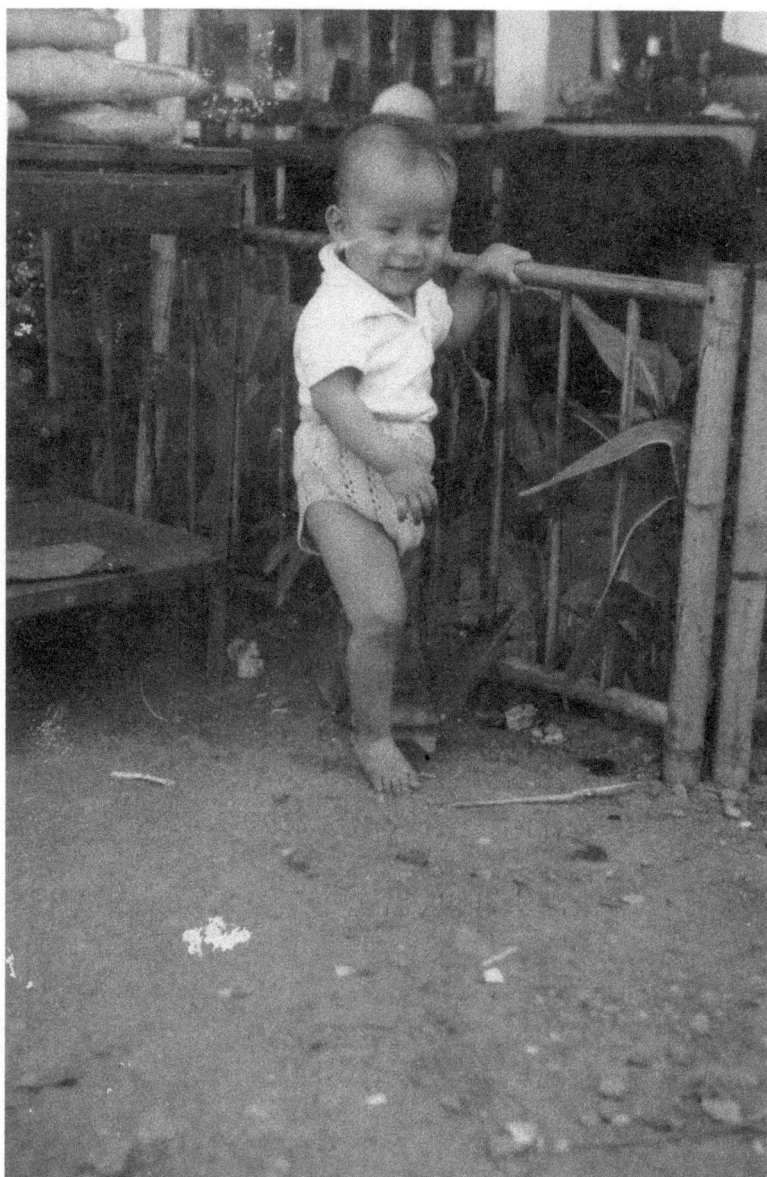

Little brother, table with bread

The house in Bay Hien Village where my dad died

Grandma, Dad, Uncle

Parents' wedding picture

ABOOKS

ALIVE Book Publishing and ALIVE Publishing Group
are imprints of Advanced Publishing LLC,
3200 A Danville Blvd., Suite 204, Alamo, California 94507

Telephone: 925.837.7303
alivebookpublishing.com

www.ingramcontent.com/pod-product-compliance
Lightning Source LLC
Chambersburg PA
CBHW022009080426
42733CB00007B/533